LOGIC
PUZZLES

BLETCHLEYPARK

This edition was published in 2017 by the Bletchley Park Trust The Mansion, Bletchley Park, Milton Keynes, MK3 6EB

ISBN: 978-1-78404-411-4
AD004279NT

Cover design by Rose
Printed in the UK

CONTENTS

INTRODUCTION

During World War Two, Bletchley Park was a workplace to thousands of people whose job it was to read the encrypted messages of its enemies. Towards the end of 1941, a crossword puzzle competition was organised by the Daily Telegraph. The challenge was to complete the puzzle in under 12 minutes. A Mr Gavin, Chairman of the Eccentrics Club offered to donate £100 to the Minesweepers Fund, if it could be done under controlled conditions. As a number of the competitors were subsequently invited to take part in intelligence work at Bletchley Park, puzzles and Codebreaking have been linked in the public mind ever since the exploits of Bletchley Park's Codebreakers became public knowledge.

Codebreaking is very much a puzzle solving process and the codes and ciphers used are similar to the most common types of puzzles such as crosswords, word searches and sudoku. In many cases, the Codebreakers of Bletchley Park were looking for patterns in the problem before them, much like puzzle solvers today. Both often also base their solutions on clues. For example, a simple code might represent words by something else such as strings of numbers. In this case, the clue may lie in the frequency of certain strings of numbers occurring in the encrypted message. Straight or quick crossword clues are simple definitions of the answers so the clue lies in the definition provided. A more difficult cipher might replace each letter in a message with another letter of the alphabet twice, a so-called double-encryption. This is a bit like cryptic crosswords in which the clues are puzzles in themselves.

Encrypted WW2 enemy messages were usually transmitted in groups of letters, typically 4 or 5 in length. So when the letters were decrypted, they would still be in these letter groups but some letters might be missing. The Codebreakers would then have to piece the actual words of the message together. This is a bit like a 'fill-in-the-blank' clue in crosswords or word search puzzles.

So you see puzzle solving is synonymous with the profound intellectual feat and remarkable brains of those whose work at Bletchley Park is said to have helped shorten WW2 by up to two years. Following in this long-held tradition, the Bletchley Park Trust has today produced this series of Puzzle Books so that you can follow in the footsteps of the Codebreakers and perhaps establish whether you have the puzzle solving skills needed to have worked at wartime Bletchley Park...

Where Do They Live?

Four friends live in the houses you see on the map below. Each is of a different age and has a different occupation. Can you piece together the facts from the information in the clues and work out where they all live?

1   Katie is one year older than the artist, who is one year older than the person who lives at No 3.

2   Martin (who lives at No 2) is younger than the doctor, but older than Penny.

3   Penny lives directly south of the baker, who is older than Penny.

4   The person (not John) who lives at No 1 isn't the oldest of the four friends.

5   John isn't the teacher.

	Name				Age				Job			
	John	Katie	Martin	Penny	28	29	30	31	Artist	Baker	Doctor	Teacher
No 1												
No 2												
No 3												
No 4												
Artist												
Baker												
Doctor												
Teacher												
28												
29												
30												
31												

House	Name	Age	Job

Five friends regularly meet up to take their dogs for walks together. Can you work out the name of each person's dog, together with its breed?

1. Digger is a terrier; he doesn't belong to Mike.
2. Of the two girls, one owns Bobo and the other owns the Alsatian.
3. David's dog is called Nero.
4. Neither Mike nor David owns the poodle.
5. Neither Mike nor Joanna owns the dog called Jinx.
6. Sam isn't the spaniel.

	Bobo	Digger	Jinx	Nero	Sam	Alsatian	Collie	Poodle	Spaniel	Terrier
Alan										
David										
Joanna										
Louise										
Mike										
Alsatian										
Collie										
Poodle										
Spaniel										
Terrier										

(Dog's Name: Bobo, Digger, Jinx, Nero, Sam — Breed: Alsatian, Collie, Poodle, Spaniel, Terrier)

Friend	Dog	Breed

Veronica's Visitors

On each of five afternoons last week, Veronica received a visit from one of her five neighbours, who arrived with a small gift for her. Which woman visited on each of the listed afternoons and what did she bring?

1 Brenda visited Veronica the day after the woman who baked a cake, but two days before the one who brought her a magazine.

2 Mary visited Veronica two days after the woman who brought a jar of honey, who called on Veronica later in the week than Sharon's visit.

3 Alice arrived on Saturday afternoon, but not with a book.

	\multicolumn{5}{c}{Visitor}	\multicolumn{5}{c}{Gift}
	Alice	Brenda	Doreen	Mary	Sharon	Book	Cake	Fruit	Honey	Magazine
Monday										
Tuesday										
Thursday										
Friday										
Saturday										
Book					
Cake					
Fruit					
Honey					
Magazine					

Afternoon	Visitor	Gift

Dancing Lessons

Four couples who are very keen on ballroom dancing are taking private lessons from Philippe, a local dance teacher. Can you match the couples, together with the night of the week each has a lesson, and the dance each is keen to master?

1 Cliff (who is keen to learn the foxtrot) has lessons the night before Lesley, but the night after the couple who are perfecting their waltz.

2 Thelma (who is learning the quickstep) has lessons two nights before Sally.

3 Hope has lessons the night after Des.

4 Ray is learning to tango.

	Partner				Night				Dance			
	Hope	Lesley	Sally	Thelma	Monday	Tuesday	Wednesday	Thursday	Foxtrot	Quickstep	Tango	Waltz
Cliff												
Des												
John												
Ray												
Foxtrot												
Quickstep												
Tango												
Waltz												
Monday												
Tuesday												
Wednesday												
Thursday												

Man	Partner	Night	Dance

Cinema Story

Four young couples went to the cinema, each on successive evenings. Can you match the names of each pair who went out on each evening, and say what type of movie they saw?

1 Sam and Kathryn went to the cinema the evening before Julia and her boyfriend did so, but the evening after the couple who saw the western.

2 Hal and his girlfriend went to the cinema the evening after the thriller was screened which, in turn, was the evening after one couple viewed the tear-jerking romance.

3 Mike went to the cinema later in the week than Lorna.

	Boyfriend				Girlfriend				Movie			
	Hal	Lester	Mike	Sam	Julia	Kathryn	Lorna	Meryl	Romance	Sci-fi	Thriller	Western
Tuesday												
Wednesday												
Thursday												
Friday												
Romance												
Sci-fi												
Thriller												
Western												
Julia												
Kathryn												
Lorna												
Meryl												

Evening	B/friend	G/friend	Movie

Captains' Reunion

At a recent college reunion, five men got chatting after they discovered each had been captain of one of the college's sports teams. In which sport and in which year did each man captain the team?

1. One of the men had captained the college badminton team two years later than the man who captained the archery team.

2. Henry's passion is hockey: he led his team throughout the year following Joe's time as a sports captain.

3. Dean led the college swimming club to many victories over teams from rival colleges, in an earlier year than Frank's captaincy.

4. Peter (who was a team captain in 2003) has never shown any interest in baseball or archery.

Captain	Sport	Year

Parcel Poser

Patsy has five parcels lined up (as you see below), but she isn't opening any until tomorrow, her birthday. You, however, can discover their contents today (together with the name of the aunt or uncle the gift is from), just by unravelling the information in the clues.

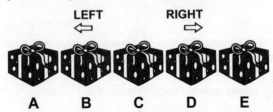

1   The parcel from Aunt Debbie is next to and right of the one containing a book, which is further right than the parcel from Patsy's Uncle Pete.

2   The parcel from Uncle Jim is next to and between two other presents, both given by aunts.

3   The parcel containing a wristwatch (not a gift from Uncle Pete) is next to and left of Aunt Lily's gift (which isn't in parcel D).

4   Parcel A doesn't contain the make-up, which is a gift from Aunt Ann. Parcel E doesn't contain the purse.

	Gift					Donor				
	Book	Clock	Make-up	Purse	Wristwatch	Aunt Ann	Aunt Debbie	Aunt Lily	Uncle Jim	Uncle Pete
Parcel A										
Parcel B										
Parcel C										
Parcel D										
Parcel E										
Aunt Ann										
Aunt Debbie										
Aunt Lily										
Uncle Jim										
Uncle Pete										

Parcel	Gift	Donor

Rushed Reports

Rob Rushmore is a television news reporter whose assignments next week include four interviews with famous people. Can you investigate the story in these clues, to discover the day and time he is scheduled to meet each, as well as the occupation of each interviewee?

1. Rob's appointment with Frank Fair is at a time of day one hour earlier than his appointment with the famous ballet dancer, who is booked to start a tour of the country next month.
2. Gina Gold was able to find time in her diary to speak to Rob on Wednesday.
3. The famous football player will be interviewed at two o'clock the day after Rob sees Dora Dean, whose interview will take place in the morning.
4. Ed Evans is coming in to the studio to be interviewed (but not in the afternoon) at an earlier time of day than Rob's appointment with the singer.

	Day				Time				Occupation			
	Tuesday	Wednesday	Thursday	Friday	10.00am	11.00am	2.00pm	3.00pm	Dancer	Footballer	Singer	Writer
Dora Dean												
Ed Evans												
Frank Fair												
Gina Gold												
Dancer												
Footballer												
Singer												
Writer												
10.00am												
11.00am												
2.00pm												
3.00pm												

Name	Day	Time	Occ'n

Split Personalities

In a bad mood at certain comments in her school report, Sarah has cut photographs of four of her teachers each into four pieces (head, body, legs and feet) and then reassembled them in such a way that each 'new' picture contains pieces of four 'old' ones. How have the pictures been reassembled?

1 Miss Givins' body is now attached to Mr Trick's legs.

2 Mrs Nuffin's feet are in the same picture as Miss Fortune's head, which is in a different picture to the legs belonging to Mr Trick.

3 Miss Givins' feet are in a different picture than Mrs Nuffin's legs.

		Body				Legs				Feet			
		Miss Fortune	Miss Givins	Mrs Nuffin	Mr Trick	Miss Fortune	Miss Givins	Mrs Nuffin	Mr Trick	Miss Fortune	Miss Givins	Mrs Nuffin	Mr Trick
Head	Miss Fortune												
	Miss Givins												
	Mrs Nuffin												
	Mr Trick												
Feet	Miss Fortune												
	Miss Givins												
	Mrs Nuffin												
	Mr Trick												
Legs	Miss Fortune												
	Miss Givins												
	Mrs Nuffin												
	Mr Trick												

Head	Body	Legs	Feet

School Essays

Five children, who took vacations abroad with their parents last semester, have all been asked by their teacher to write short essays on their trips. How many words has each written and which country did he or she visit?

1. Arnie has written 30 more words than the girl who visited India with her parents.
2. The child who went to Japan has written ten fewer words than Bella.
3. Saul's essay on Holland mainly concerns the windmills he saw there.
4. The essay precisely 110 words in length was penned by Gemma.
5. Douglas has written 20 fewer words than the child who enjoyed a vacation in Antigua.

	Length					Visited				
	90 words	100 words	110 words	120 words	130 words	Antigua	France	Holland	India	Japan
Arnie										
Bella										
Douglas										
Gemma										
Saul										
Antigua										
France										
Holland										
India										
Japan										

Child	Length	Visited

Patchwork Pony

Patricia has made a patchwork pony for her son to play with, using scraps of old material. Every piece was made on a different day last week – but can you piece together the details from the clues below?

1   The tail of the pony was made (from the ruffle of a no-longer-fashionable blouse of Patricia's) two days after the head was made, but earlier in the week than the part of the pony which used material from an old curtain.

2   A torn shirt of Patricia's husband's was used for the piece made on Tuesday.

3   The hind legs of the pony were made the day after Patricia had cut up a pair of her husband's old trousers, but earlier in the week than the forelegs were made.

	Piece					Material				
	Body	Forelegs	Head	Hind legs	Tail	Blouse	Curtain	Jacket	Shirt	Trousers
Tuesday										
Wednesday										
Thursday										
Friday										
Saturday										
Blouse										
Curtain										
Jacket										
Shirt										
Trousers										

Day	Piece	Material

Knitted Gifts

Babs has just finished knitting four garments, one for each of her four grandchildren, whose mothers are the daughters of Babs. Which child will receive each garment, who is his or her mother and what are the children's ages?

1 Connor is older than Daphne's child, but younger than the child for whom Babs has knitted a hat.

2 Flora's child is older than the one who will receive a pair of mittens, but younger than Felix, who won't be receiving the hat.

3 Martine is older than the child for whom Babs has knitted a colourful scarf, but younger than Chrissie's child.

4 The scarf isn't a gift for Daphne's child.

5 The hat isn't a gift for Flora's child.

	Child				Mother				Age			
	Connor	Deanna	Felix	Martine	Chrissie	Daphne	Flora	Mary	4	5	6	7
Hat												
Mittens												
Scarf												
Sweater												
4												
5												
6												
7												
Chrissie												
Daphne												
Flora												
Mary												

Garment	Child	Mother	Age

A Family Matter

Each of the four families in this puzzle consists of a husband, wife, son and daughter, whose names begin with four different letters of the alphabet. Can you determine who is related to whom?

1 Brian's mother has a name which starts with the same letter as the name of Charlie's sister.

2 Austin's wife has a name which starts with the same letter as the name of Doreen's husband.

3 Andy's sister has a name which starts with the same letter as the name of Brian's father.

4 Angela's son has a name which starts with the same letter as the name of Dave's mother.

		Wife				Son				Daughter			
		Angela	Brenda	Camilla	Doreen	Andy	Brian	Charlie	Dave	Alison	Barbara	Clarissa	Dawn
Husband	Austin												
	Bill												
	Clive												
	Douglas												
Daughter	Alison												
	Barbara												
	Clarissa												
	Dawn												
Son	Andy												
	Brian												
	Charlie												
	Dave												

Husband	Wife	Son	Daughter

Love-Hate Relationship

Mealtimes can be slightly difficult in the household of the Cook family, as each of Mr and Mrs Cook's five children loves a particular vegetable which is hated by one of their other children. Digest the clues below to find out who loves and hates each of the listed vegetables.

1. The child who loves peas really detests the vegetable that Dennis adores; and Dennis hates the vegetable (not beans) that Lynda adores.

2. Lynda hates the vegetable that Mark loves; and Mark hates the vegetable that Carla prefers to all others.

3. Jane hates cabbage, however it is cooked.

4. The child who loves beans hates carrots.

	Loves					Hates				
	Beans	Cabbage	Carrots	Peas	Turnips	Beans	Cabbage	Carrots	Peas	Turnips
Carla										
Dennis										
Jane										
Lynda										
Mark										
Hates Beans					
Cabbage					
Carrots					
Peas					
Turnips					

Child	Loves	Hates

19

Flowers Everywhere!

When Hannah spent a few days in hospital following her recent (and successful) operation, five friends called in to visit, each on a different day, and each bearing a large bunch of flowers. Which friend visited on each of the listed days and at what time?

1   Fran's visit was the day after (and at a time four hours earlier in the day than) Judith called in to see Hannah, bearing a bunch of beautifully scented freesias.

2   Penny's visit was at a time one hour earlier than that of the woman who visited Hannah on Thursday afternoon.

3   Eva's visit was later in the day than that of the woman who visited on Wednesday, but earlier than that of the woman who visited Hannah on Friday.

	Friend					Time				
	Carolyn	Eva	Fran	Judith	Penny	10.00am	11.00am	2.00pm	3.00pm	4.00pm
Tuesday										
Wednesday										
Thursday										
Friday										
Saturday										
10.00am					
11.00am					
2.00pm					
3.00pm					
4.00pm					

Day	Friend	Time

Say Cheese!

The four people lined up in the diagram below are waiting to be served at the cheese counter in their local deli, and each wants a different cheese, from either Holland or France. Can you identify each person (name and surname) and say which cheese each is about to buy?

1 There is just one shopper standing between Karen Fox and the man waiting to buy a piece of Dutch Gouda.

2 The person who wants a wedge of creamy Camembert isn't Maxine.

3 The shopper identified by the letter B in the diagram below is waiting to buy a piece of French Brie.

4 Rory isn't the person surnamed Grove, who is identified by the letter C in the diagram.

5 The customer surnamed Watson isn't Barry, who is furthest right in the diagram.

	Barry	Karen	Maxine	Rory	Fox	Grove	O'Brien	Watson	Brie	Camembert	Edam	Gouda
Person A												
Person B												
Person C												
Person D												
Brie								
Camembert								
Edam								
Gouda								
Fox				
Grove				
O'Brien				
Watson				

LEFT ⇦   **RIGHT** ⇨

A B C D

Person	Name	Surname	Cheese

Chocolate Drops

Four children were each given a bag of chocolate drops, and began chomping their way through them about ten minutes ago. Before they resume eating, can you discover how many dark chocolate, milk chocolate and white chocolate drops remain in each child's bag?

1   The child with nine dark chocolate drops has two more white chocolates than Pippa, who has two more milk chocolate drops than Callum (who isn't the child with nine dark chocolate drops).

2   The child with the fewest milk chocolates has four fewer white chocolate drops than Sean, who has two fewer milk chocolates than Jasmine.

3   Jasmine has one more dark chocolate than white chocolate drops.

4   The child with the fewest white chocolate drops doesn't have the fewest dark chocolate drops.

	Dark	Milk	White
	7 8 9 10	4 6 8 10	3 5 7 9
Callum			
Jasmine			
Pippa			
Sean			
White 3			
5			
7			
9			
Milk 4			
6			
8			
10			

Child	Dark	Milk	White

There is a murder for Inspector Porritt to solve in and around the small village of Benthorn, in each episode of the long-running TV series *The Benthorn Murders*. Can you investigate all of the clues to decide the order in which the five listed people met their deaths, together with the murder weapon in every case?

1   The third victim was hit by a rock thrown from a balcony.

2   The brakes were tampered with in Chloë Dean's car, causing her to plunge to her death over the edge of a mountain road. She wasn't the first nor the last of the five people to die.

3   The fifth person to die was neither Alf Barnet nor the person who was poisoned.

4   Bob Cole's murder was investigated by Inspector Porritt earlier than the case involving the poisoning of one of the victims.

5   Dan Elder's murder directly followed that of the person who was shot.

	First	Second	Third	Fourth	Fifth	Automobile	Gun	Knife	Poison	Rock
Alf Barnet										
Bob Cole										
Chloë Dean										
Dan Elder										
Emma Fry										
Automobile										
Gun										
Knife										
Poison										
Rock										

Victim	Order	Weapon

Island Worshippers

Hidden away in the middle of an ocean, surrounded by hundreds of miles of water, is the island of Elusiva, only recently discovered by the rest of mankind! It is inhabited by five different tribes who occupy the territories as marked on the map below. Over the years, each tribe has discovered an object on the beach, which is now revered as a holy gift from their Great God, Leevusalone. Do some discovering yourself... Work out the facts from these clues.

1 The Bule tribe lives further west than the tribe whose chief's wife discovered the oildrum.
2 The canoe paddle was discovered on the beach belonging to the Tupin, who live further west than the Fora tribe (which doesn't live in the area marked A on the map).
3 The chief of the Conji tribe discovered an old shoe, which he feels proves that the Great God has only one leg.
4 The airbed was found by the tribe which lives in the territory next to and north of the area in which the Yalom tribe lives.
5 The beachball wasn't found by the tribe which lives in the territory marked B on the map.

	Bule	Conji	Fora	Tupin	Yalom	Airbed	Beachball	Canoe paddle	Oildrum	Shoe
Territory A										
Territory B										
Territory C										
Territory D										
Territory E										
Airbed										
Beachball										
Canoe paddle										
Oildrum										
Shoe										

Territory	Tribe	Gift

Wedding Bells

Four cousins got married in the latter part of last year. What is each one's surname, to whom is he married, and when did they wed?

1 Ritchie married two months later than Mr and Mrs Rook, neither of whom is Thomas or Leanne (who isn't married to Ritchie).

2 Leanne married the month after Carol, but earlier in the year than Mr and Mrs Green.

3 Daniel married the month before Rosa Ward.

	Surname				Wife				Month			
	Baker	Green	Rook	Ward	Carol	Leanne	Rosa	Suzi	August	September	October	December
Daniel												
Martin												
Ritchie												
Thomas												
August												
September												
October												
December												
Carol												
Leanne												
Rosa												
Suzi												

Cousin	Surname	Wife	Month

Diving for Gold

Four friends who are keen divers joined different parties of explorers last summer, in search of sunken ships reported to be laden with gold. However, none found gold, although they did manage to locate the vessels they were searching for and bring up some cargo. Dive through the clues below to discover which vessel each friend explored, the year in which it sank, and its cargo.

1   There was silver (but not a lot of it!) in the hold of the ship which sank 40 years before the one to which Benjamin dived. Benjamin's party didn't explore the *Fontaine* (which sank in a later year than the *Lucy Jane*).

2   The guns found by the party Pamela joined were in too poor a condition to be of any value other than mementos of the trip.

3   Robert was with the team that located the ship containing cases of pottery, which sank earlier than that carrying a cargo of rum, but later than the *Warwick*.

4   The *Barbera* disappeared beneath the waves in August 1902.

	Barbera	Fontaine	Lucy Jane	Warwick	1862	1882	1902	1922	Guns	Pottery	Rum	Silver
Benjamin												
Fiona												
Pamela												
Robert												
Guns												
Pottery												
Rum												
Silver												
1862												
1882												
1902												
1922												

Friend	Vessel	Sank	Cargo

Join the Party

Lou received five invitations in the post today, all asking him to different parties being held next month. What event is being celebrated on each of the listed dates, and what is the name of the person organizing the party?

1   Helen has just moved into a new house. Her house-warming party will take place earlier in the month than Greta's party, but later in the month than that being held to celebrate someone's graduation from college.

2   The birthday party is being held six days later than Isabel's party, which isn't to celebrate a graduation or retirement. Greta isn't organizing the birthday party.

3   The person throwing a surprise wedding anniversary event for his or her parents has arranged it on a date earlier in the month than Tim's party, which isn't arranged for the 29th of next month.

	Event					Name				
	Anniversary	Birthday	Graduation	New house	Retirement	Donald	Greta	Helen	Isabel	Tim
8th										
13th										
19th										
23rd										
29th										
Donald										
Greta										
Helen										
Isabel										
Tim										

Date	Event	Name

The Highwaymen

In England, during the mid-1700s, five brothers operated as highwaymen, apprehending travellers and robbing them of their goods and possessions. By 1782, the last of the five had been captured, and the roads were (for a while) safe again. Each had a favourite steed and operated in an area near to a different town. Journey through the clues to see if you can discover the name of every brother's horse and the town whose highways he terrorized.

1 Bold Bill often robbed merchants travelling to the weekly market at Northwood. He was captured earlier than the man who rode Brown Bess, who didn't rob anyone in the roads leading to and from Appleford.

2 Fearless Frank's steed was neither Brown Bess nor Lightning.

3 Lightning's rider (who operated in the area of Sandbridge) wasn't Daring Dan. Daring Dan didn't ply his evil trade near the town of Bunbury.

4 Storm was ridden by Artful Al, until he was captured in 1779.

5 Moonbeam wasn't ridden by Fearless Frank, who didn't operate near the town of Appleford.

	Horse					Town				
	Brown Bess	Fleetfoot	Lightning	Moonbeam	Storm	Appleford	Bunbury	Northwood	Oakton	Sandbridge
Artful Al										
Bold Bill										
Daring Dan										
Evil Edmund										
Fearless Frank										
Appleford										
Bunbury										
Northwood										
Oakton										
Sandbridge										

Brother	Horse	Town

Playing Cards

The four men in this puzzle are playing a game of cards and each has three in his hand: one heart, one club and one diamond. Can you discover which three cards are in each man's hand? (NB – A=ace, J=jack, Q=queen and K=king; and in the game, ace=1, jack=11, queen=12, king=13 and the values of the other cards are as per their numbers.)

1 Eric's heart has a higher value than that of Ken's diamond.

2 The man with the six of clubs and the queen of diamonds is holding a heart with a value three lower than that of Roy's club.

3 The man (not Eric) holding both the jack of hearts and the jack of clubs has a diamond with a lower value than that of Eric's club.

4 The man with the five of hearts isn't holding the king of diamonds.

		Heart				Club				Diamond			
		A	5	J	Q	4	6	8	J	5	8	Q	K
	Eric												
	Ken												
	Patrick												
	Roy												
Diamond	5												
	8												
	Q												
	K												
Club	4												
	6												
	8												
	J												

Player	Heart	Club	Diamond

29

Tradesmen

Four tradesmen are currently working at addresses locally – and no tradesman has a surname which coincides with his profession. Can you work out not only the occupation of each, but also the name of his client and the address at which each tradesman is working?

1   Joe Painter's client is Mrs Farmer, the tiler is working for Mr Smith, and Mr Butcher lives in Wood Way.

2   Andy Joiner is working in Copper Lane. He isn't the painter.

3   Mark Plumber isn't the joiner, who is currently working in Slate Street.

4   Miss Baker doesn't live in Brick Road. Sam Tiler's client isn't Miss Baker.

	Trade				Client				Address			
	Joiner	Painter	Plumber	Tiler	Miss Baker	Mr Butcher	Mrs Farmer	Mr Smith	Brick Road	Copper Lane	Slate Street	Wood Way
Andy Joiner												
Joe Painter												
Mark Plumber												
Sam Tiler												
Brick Road												
Copper Lane												
Slate Street												
Wood Way												
Miss Baker												
Mr Butcher												
Mrs Farmer												
Mr Smith												

Name	Trade	Client	Address

Celebrity Openings

The Pricelow supermarket chain is opening five new stores across the country next week, and each store has hired a celebrity to promote the event by cutting a ribbon at the main entrance. Can you discover the occupation of each celebrity, together with the day on which he or she is booked to open a store?

1   Dale Drew is opening a store two days later than the movie director, but earlier in the week than the author has been booked to appear.

2   Will Walters is an actor. He's due to open a supermarket later in the week than Fionna Finn's booking (which isn't scheduled to take place on Monday).

3   Sue Sheldon is opening a store on Thursday.

4   The singer isn't due to open a store on Wednesday.

	Occupation					Opening day				
	Actor	Author	Hockey player	Movie director	Singer	Monday	Tuesday	Wednesday	Thursday	Friday
Dale Drew										
Fionna Finn										
Polly Piper										
Sue Sheldon										
Will Walters										
Monday					
Tuesday					
Wednesday					
Thursday					
Friday					

Celebrity	Occupation	Opening

Stately Surnames

Coincidentally, Sue and her siblings all married men with rather stately sounding surnames! Can you link each sister to her partner and their somewhat grand surname?

1 The woman married to Adam King isn't Maggie, who is older than Beryl.

2 Tammy Earl's husband isn't Keith.

3 Beryl's youngest sister is married to Barry Duke.

4 Beryl lives next door to Sue and her husband Wayne, whose surname isn't Prince.

		Husband					Surname				
	Adam	Barry	Keith	Rob	Wayne	Duke	Earl	King	Lord	Prince
Beryl										
Lorraine										
Maggie										
Sue										
Tammy										
Duke										
Earl										
King										
Lord										
Prince										

Sister	Husband	Surname

Family Picture

Dave and Kate have four children, all of whom are depicted in the photograph below. Each is of a different age and has a different hair colour to the others (something which is not unusual in either Dave's or Kate's families). Can you identify each child in the picture?

1   Lisa has blonde hair. She's standing further left than the child who is two years younger than Nicholas.

2   The 11-year-old has a beautiful head of ginger hair and is standing further right than Damien.

3   Jane is one year older than the child with light brown hair, who is further left than (and not directly next to) Damien.

		Damien	Jane	Lisa	Nicholas	8	10	11	12	Black	Blonde	Brown	Ginger
	Child 1												
	Child 2												
	Child 3												
	Child 4												
Hair	Black												
	Blonde												
	Brown												
	Ginger												
Age	8												
	10												
	11												
	12												

LEFT ⇐   **RIGHT** ⇒

Child	Name	Age	Hair

Collages

Four children have made collages, using different quantities of fern fronds, leaves and flower petals. How many of each did every child use to make his or her picture?

1 Boris used the same number of leaves as fern fronds, which was higher than the number of petals in his collage.

2 George used more petals than ferns, but not two more ferns than leaves.

3 The quantity of leaves used by Marie was the same as the number of petals used by Diana.

4 The child who used five leaves also used eight petals. The one who used eight ferns also used seven petals.

	Ferns				Leaves				Petals			
	6	7	8	9	4	5	6	7	5	6	7	8
Boris												
Diana												
George												
Marie												
Petals 5												
6												
7												
8												
Leaves 4												
5												
6												
7												

Child	Ferns	Leaves	Petals

Split Personalities

Little Lynne has used her scissors on pictures of her five older brothers and sisters, cutting each into three pieces (head, body and legs) and then reassembling them in such a way that each 'new' photograph contains pieces of three 'old' ones. How have the pictures been reassembled?

1 Louise's head is not in the same picture as Christina's body.

2 David's legs and Hannah's body are in two different pictures.

3 Hannah's head is in the same picture as Christina's legs, but not David's body.

4 David's head is not in the same picture as Louise's legs, which are now attached to Philip's body.

		Body					Legs				
		Christina	David	Hannah	Louise	Philip	Christina	David	Hannah	Louise	Philip
Head	Christina										
	David										
	Hannah										
	Louise										
	Philip										
Legs	Christina										
	David										
	Hannah										
	Louise										
	Philip										

Head	Body	Legs

Sail Away

At the jetty (see map below) on the shores of Lake Laverne are five boats, each of which has been hired for different lengths of time by different families who wish to explore the lake and surrounding woodlands. Before they sail away, can you discover the surname of the family in each boat, together with the period for which it has been hired?

1   The Dunn family has hired a boat for two fewer days than the Hooper family, whose boat is moored further south and further west than the one in which the Wallace family is about to sail away.

2   The family which has hired a boat for the longest period is in the vessel moored directly south of that hired by the Fisher family, which is further east than the boat hired for the shortest period.

3   Boat B has been hired for five more days than boat A.

4   The Wallace family will be sailing for a shorter period than the Taylor family.

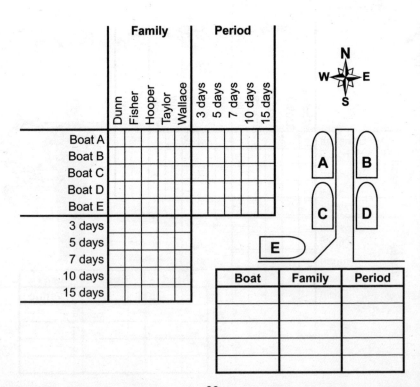

The four boys in this puzzle are all taking out girls tonight – the first time any of them (including the girls) has ever been on a date with a member of the opposite sex. Who has each boy asked out, at what time will they meet, and where are they going?

1   Roberta is meeting her date fifteen minutes later than the time agreed by Ronnie and his date, and half an hour later than the couple who are going for a meal at the Italian restaurant in town.

2   Darren is meeting his date fifteen minutes later than the time at which the couple who are going to the dance have arranged to meet, and half an hour later than the time agreed by Nadine and her date.

3   The couple who are going to the cinema are meeting fifteen minutes later than the time agreed by Amber and her date, and half an hour later than the time arranged between Laurence and his date.

4   Neil and his date have arranged to meet later than seven o'clock.

	Amber	Juliet	Nadine	Roberta	7.00pm	7.15pm	7.30pm	7.45pm	Bowling	Cinema	Dance	Restaurant
Darren												
Laurence												
Neil												
Ronnie												
Bowling								
Cinema								
Dance								
Restaurant								
7.00pm				
7.15pm				
7.30pm				
7.45pm				

Boy	Girl	Time	Venue

Lucy's Lunches

Lucy always takes a packed lunch to work. It invariably consists of a slice of home-made cake, a piece of fruit and a sandwich. She wasn't in the office last Tuesday, so can you work through the clues to discover what she ate on each of the other four days last week?

1   The lunch of a slice of coconut cake followed by a pear was eaten later in the week than the sliced beef sandwich (which wasn't eaten on the same day as the chocolate cake).

2   Lucy followed her Canadian cheddar cheese sandwich with a banana one day. This was earlier in the week than she ate raisin cake (which wasn't in her lunchbox on Friday).

3   The ham sandwich wasn't eaten on the same day as the orange, which formed part of Lucy's lunch the day after she packed a slice of chocolate cake in her lunchbox.

4   The beef sandwich and the orange were eaten on different days last week.

	Cake				Fruit				Sandwich			
	Chocolate	Coconut	Ginger	Raisin	Apple	Banana	Orange	Pear	Beef	Cheese	Ham	Salad
Monday												
Wednesday												
Thursday												
Friday												
Beef								
Cheese								
Ham								
Salad								
Apple				
Banana				
Orange				
Pear				

Day	Cake	Fruit	Sandwich

Janet and John

In the hamlet of Elkwood live five family groups in which there is one girl named Janet and one boy named John. Luckily each family has a different surname and all ten children are of different ages! Can you match each brother-sister pair, by age, to their family name?

1. John Brown is one year younger than his sister Janet.
2. Janet Courtney is three years older than her brother.
3. The boy aged ten has a sister aged seven.
4. Janet Weller is the youngest of the five girls.
5. John Gorman is one year older than the brother of the eight-year-old girl.

	Janet (age)					John (age)				
	4	7	8	9	12	3	5	6	10	11
Atkinson										
Brown										
Courtney										
Gorman										
Weller										
John (age) 3										
5										
6										
10										
11										

Surname	Janet	John

Mothers' Race

Five mothers took part in the local school's sports day mothers' race. Can you work out who ran in each of the lanes marked on the plan below, as well as her finishing position?

1　Lee ran in a lane with a number one lower than that of the mother who came last in the race.

2　The woman who ran in lane 3 finished one place behind Debbie, but one place ahead of the woman who ran in lane 5.

3　Caroline finished later in the race than Sharon, who ran in a lane with a number two higher than that of the mother who came first.

4　The woman in lane 2 didn't finish first or last in the race.

	Caroline	Debbie	Lee	Sharon	Toni	First	Second	Third	Fourth	Fifth
Lane 1										
Lane 2										
Lane 3										
Lane 4										
Lane 5										
First										
Second										
Third										
Fourth										
Fifth										

FINISH

1	2	3	4	5

START

Lane	Mother	Finished

Much Ado!

36

Prior to Peter Perfect joining the cast in 2010, different actors played the part of Romeo in the Footlights Theatre Company's production of Shakespeare's *Romeo and Juliet*, each being replaced for a different reason. Can you discover each actor's full name, the year in which he played Romeo and the reason he was dismissed that year?

1 Dick Duke played the part of Romeo later than the man (not Dean) dismissed for constantly throwing tantrums off-stage.

2 Dean Doran isn't the man who was dismissed for drunkenness. The man dismissed for drunkenness left the cast earlier than 2010.

3 Doug played the rôle the year before Mr Dance, who had to go because he frequently forgot his lines.

	Dance	Derby	Doran	Duke	2007	2008	2009	2010	Absenteeism	Drunkenness	Forgot lines	Tantrums
Dave												
Dean												
Dick												
Doug												
Absenteeism												
Drunkenness												
Forgot lines												
Tantrums												
2007												
2008												
2009												
2010												

Actor	Surname	Year	Reason

41

Christmas Cards

Each of the four people who appear in this puzzle bought more cards than they needed last Christmas. Can you discover how many every person bought and sent, and how many each received from other people?

1   The person who bought the most Christmas cards didn't send three more than he or she received.

2   The person who received the fewest Christmas cards sent one fewer than Noelle and bought five fewer than Stephen.

3   Stephen sent one fewer than were sent by Emmanuel.

4   Gloria bought ten fewer Christmas cards and received two more than Emmanuel.

5   The person who received 23 Christmas cards didn't send 25 cards.

	Bought				Sent				Received			
	30	35	40	45	25	26	27	28	21	22	23	24
Emmanuel												
Gloria												
Noelle												
Stephen												
Received 21												
22												
23												
24												
Sent 25												
26												
27												
28												

Name	Bought	Sent	Received

Backing Singers

The Voicettes are a backing group frequently hired by BNI Records to accompany solo singers making recordings. Every day last week (Monday to Friday) The Voicettes were in the BNI Studio with a different artist. Can you work out who they sang with each day, together with the title of the song in each case?

1   Fiona Fay made her recording earlier in the week than Gina Gould, who The Voicettes accompanied the day before providing the backing to *Losing You*.

2   The Voicettes backed the rather repetitive song *My Dream* earlier in the week than they accompanied Ed Engles, which was earlier in the week than the day on which they sang *Only You*.

3   Dave Dyme was in the BNI Studio earlier in the week than the artiste who recorded *No, No, No*, who was in the BNI Studio earlier in the week than the person who sang *Keep Cool*.

4   The person who sang *Keep Cool* was backed by The Voicettes either the day before or the day after they sang with Harry Hibbert.

	Dave Dyme	Ed Engles	Fiona Fay	Gina Gould	Harry Hibbert	Keep Cool	Losing You	My Dream	No, No, No	Only You
Monday										
Tuesday										
Wednesday										
Thursday										
Friday										
Keep Cool										
Losing You										
My Dream										
No, No, No										
Only You										

Day	Singer	Song

39   Train Crazy

Terry is crazy about old steam engines. Last year, on a tour of Britain, he managed to travel on five different trains. Can you discover, in the order he travelled, the name of the locomotive pulling each train, and the place at which he took a photograph?

1. *Foxcote Manor* pulled the train Terry travelled on directly after the one from which he took a picture of the beautiful Severn Valley, which was earlier than the picture he took of Levisham station whilst on a train pulled by *Sir Nigel Gresley*.

2. The Hall Class 4-6-0 locomotive, *Kinlet Hall* pulled the final train on which Terry rode on his tour, from which he took neither the photograph of picturesque Llangollen station nor that of Arley. The first picture wasn't taken at Llangollen.

3. The photograph of Arley was taken later than the picture Terry took whilst on the train pulled by Manor Class No 7812 *Erlestoke Manor*.

4. The picture of Levisham station was taken directly before that of Ramsbottom station.

5. The picture taken of Llangollen wasn't that taken whilst on board the train pulled by *King Edward I*.

	Locomotive					Place				
	Erlestoke Manor	Foxcote Manor	Kinlet Hall	King Edward I	Sir Nigel Gresley	Arley	Levisham	Llangollen	Ramsbottom	Severn Valley
First										
Second										
Third										
Fourth										
Fifth										
Arley										
Levisham										
Llangollen										
Ramsbottom										
Severn Valley										

Order	Locomotive	Place

44

Four sisters of different ages brush their teeth using different toothpastes. Every girl has a toothbrush of a different colour, so see if you can find out the age of each sister, together with the toothpaste she uses and the colour of her toothbrush.

1   The girl who prefers Fresh Mint toothpaste is two years younger than Michelle, who is either one year older or one year younger than the girl who uses the red toothbrush.

2   Trudi (who brushes with Ice Mint toothpaste) is one year older than the girl who has a yellow toothbrush.

3   Claire's toothbrush is white. Claire is older than the girl who prefers to brush her teeth with Mild Mint toothpaste.

	Age				Toothpaste				Toothbrush			
	8	10	11	12	Cool Mint	Fresh Mint	Ice Mint	Mild Mint	Blue	Red	White	Yellow
Claire												
Frances												
Michelle												
Trudi												
Blue												
Red												
White												
Yellow												
Cool Mint												
Fresh Mint												
Ice Mint												
Mild Mint												

Sister	Age	Toothpaste	Toothbrush

Colour Conundrum

The four women in this puzzle are each wearing a blouse and skirt in two different colours. No woman has a name which starts with the same letter as that of her surname, so study the clues to find out every woman's full name, together with the colour of the blouse and skirt she is wearing.

1   The colour of Miss White's blouse is the same as the colour of the skirt Beth is wearing.

2   Gina isn't the woman wearing a brown blouse and black skirt.

3   Barbara's surname starts with a different letter to that of the colour of the blouse which Gina is wearing.

4   Mrs Black's skirt is brown and Miss Green's blouse is black.

	Surname				Blouse				Skirt			
	Black	Brown	Green	White	Black	Brown	Green	White	Black	Brown	Green	White
Barbara												
Beth												
Gina												
Wendy												
Skirt Black												
Brown												
Green												
White												
Blouse Black												
Brown												
Green												
White												

Name	Surname	Blouse	Skirt

Parking Problem

The owners of the five cars parked in the lot depicted below all work for the same company. Who owns each vehicle and what is his or her position in the company?

1 The person who works as a clerk is parked due north of the car owned by the receptionist.

2 Dinah's car is parked next to (either due east or due west of) that owned by the clerk.

3 The manager's car is directly next to and west of that belonging to the janitor, whose car is directly north of Elizabeth's.

4 Richard's car is further north and further west than Mike's vehicle.

	Owner					Position				
	Dinah	Elizabeth	Mike	Richard	Terence	Accountant	Clerk	Janitor	Manager	Receptionist
Car 1										
Car 2										
Car 3										
Car 4										
Car 5										
Accountant					
Clerk					
Janitor					
Manager					
Receptionist					

Car	Owner	Position

Musical Bottles

George is very pleased with the musical instrument he made! He filled nine bottles with water, placing different measures in each so that, when struck, they produce different notes. However, he neglected to place them in order, so the alternate bottles (clear, plain glass) produce the notes F, A, C and E, but the rest don't produce the notes they should... See the diagram below to discover the note each bottle should produce (as shown in brackets), and use the clues below to discover the note each bottle actually produces, together with the colour of the bottle.

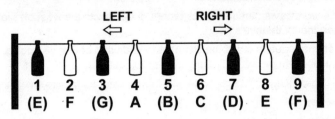

LEFT ⇐   **RIGHT** ⇒

1	2	3	4	5	6	7	8	9
(E)	F	(G)	A	(B)	C	(D)	E	(F)

1 Bottle 3 should produce the note that the brown bottle actually *does* produce.

2 The bottle which produces F when struck is further right than the purple bottle which, in turn, is further right than the yellow bottle which produces D when struck.

3 Bottle 7 produces E when struck, unlike the green bottle.

	Note actually produced					Colour				
	E	G	B	D	F	Blue	Brown	Green	Purple	Yellow
Bottle 1										
Bottle 3										
Bottle 5										
Bottle 7										
Bottle 9										
Blue										
Brown										
Green										
Purple										
Yellow										

Bottle	Note	Colour

Playing Cards

The four women in this puzzle are playing a game of cards and each has three in her hand: one heart, one club and one spade. Can you discover which three cards are in each woman's hand? (NB – A=ace, J=jack, Q=queen and K=king; and in the game, ace=1, jack=11, queen=12, king=13 and the values of the other cards are as per their numbers.)

1 Ruby isn't the woman with the queen of hearts, who has a spade with a value three higher than that of Ruby's club.

2 The woman with the jack of clubs has a heart with a value one higher than that of Jeanne's heart.

3 Gemma's club has a value three lower than that of Ruby's spade.

4 Ruby's spade has a lower value than that of her heart.

5 The woman with the jack of spades isn't holding the two of hearts in her hand.

6 Jeanne's spade hasn't a value four higher than that of Gemma's club.

		Heart				Club				Spade			
		A	2	Q	K	6	7	J	K	9	10	J	Q
	Carol												
	Gemma												
	Jeanne												
	Ruby												
Spade	9												
	10												
	J												
	Q												
Club	6												
	7												
	J												
	K												

Player	Heart	Club	Spade

Homemade Cards

Sheryl and her three friends make decorative cards for birthdays, Christmas and other occasions, selling them to their families and neighbours. Last year, the four women sold every card they made. Your task is to discover just how many of each of the three types of cards each woman made in total last year, given that each woman made three different quantities.

1 The woman who made fewest birthday cards also made one fewer 'other' cards than Sheryl, who made one fewer birthday card than Teresa.

2 Teresa made one fewer 'other' card than the woman who made one more Christmas card than Paula (who made the fewest 'other' cards).

	Birthday				Christmas				Other			
	16	17	18	19	16	17	18	19	16	17	18	19
Paula												
Rowena												
Sheryl												
Teresa												
Other 16												
Other 17												
Other 18												
Other 19												
Christmas 16												
Christmas 17												
Christmas 18												
Christmas 19												

Name	Birthday	Christmas	Other

Lunch Breaks

Each of the five people who share an office takes it in turn to collect sandwiches for lunch, from a nearby sandwich bar, with everyone being allocated a different day of the week for the task. On any one day, there are four people in the office, as each person has a regular day off. Your task is to decide which day each person collects lunch, as well as which is his or her day off.

1 The person away from the office on Wednesday collects lunch the day before Stephanie, whose day off is the day on which William collects lunch (which isn't Monday).

2 Jenny's day off is earlier in the week than the day she collects lunch, but one day later in the week than William's day off.

3 Maurice's day off is two days later than the day he collects lunch.

4 Adam always gets the lunch on Wednesday. His day off is later in the week than that of the person who gets lunch on Tuesday.

	Lunch day					Day off				
	Monday	Tuesday	Wednesday	Thursday	Friday	Monday	Tuesday	Wednesday	Thursday	Friday
Adam										
Jenny										
Maurice										
Stephanie										
William										
Monday										
Tuesday										
Wednesday										
Thursday										
Friday										

Day off

Name	Lunch	Day off

Paint Work

Five people who live in the houses shown on the map below are currently painting their front doors in various colours. Who lives at each address and which colour has he or she decided to use?

1. The person using an eye-catching shade of yellow lives due north of Charles, whose house has a number one lower than that which is home to George.

2. The person painting his or her front door in a tasteful shade of green lives due north of the person using blue paint.

3. Janice lives due east of Emma. Janice's house has a lower number than Shane's house.

4. Charles isn't using white paint. George isn't using blue paint.

	Occupant					Colour				
	Charles	Emma	George	Janice	Shane	Blue	Green	Red	White	Yellow
No 1										
No 2										
No 7										
No 8										
No 9										
Blue										
Green										
Red										
White										
Yellow										

House No	Occupant	Colour

Artificial Flowers

A new florist shop has opened in town and has some extremely beautiful artificial flowers for sale, alongside the customary range of blooms and plants. Four women each treated themselves last week. What did each woman buy, in what quantity and on which day?

1 One woman bought two more carnations than the quantity of irises bought by another woman.

2 The irises were bought the day before Diane made her purchase. Diane bought one fewer flower than the number bought by Gemma.

3 The woman who bought flowers on Tuesday purchased fewer than Marcia, but more than the woman who bought silk roses.

4 Chris (who didn't buy the fewest flowers) made her purchase on Wednesday.

	Carnations	Irises	Poppies	Roses	3	4	5	7	Monday	Tuesday	Wednesday	Thursday
Chris												
Diane												
Gemma												
Marcia												
Monday												
Tuesday												
Wednesday												
Thursday												
3												
4												
5												
7												

Quantity

Name	Flowers	Quantity	Day

49   Christmas Crackers

Four members of the Pullen family each pulled a cracker after lunch on Christmas Day. Every cracker had a different picture on the front and contained a hat and a 'novelty' gift inside. Can you discover the facts from the clues, given that everyone ended up with the contents of his or her own cracker?

1   Of the two women: one pulled the cracker (not with the picture of a sprig of holly on the front) containing the green hat; and the other sat next to the man whose cracker contained a small pencil.

2   Of the two men: one pulled the cracker containing both a mirror and a blue hat; and the other pulled a cracker with a picture of an angel on the front.

3   Of Sharon and the person whose cracker contained the yellow hat: one pulled the cracker with a keyring inside; and the other had a cracker with a picture of Santa on the front.

4   Of the person whose cracker had a picture of a robin on the front and the one whose cracker had the red hat: one had the cracker containing a pencil; and the other is Ray.

	Angel	Holly	Robin	Santa	Blue	Green	Red	Yellow	Keyring	Mirror	Pencil	Whistle
Barry												
Louise												
Ray												
Sharon												
Keyring												
Mirror												
Pencil												
Whistle												
Blue												
Green												
Red												
Yellow												

Name	Picture	Hat	Gift

54

Split Personalities

Bored with not being able to play outside due to the rain, Maggie took photographs of five members of her family, then cut each into three pieces (head, body and legs), reassembling them in such a way that each 'new' picture contains pieces of three 'old' ones. How have the pictures been reassembled?

1   Maggie's brother's legs are now attached to the body of the person whose legs are in the same picture as Maggie's grandpa's head.

2   Her mother's head is now attached to the body of the person whose head is in the same picture as Maggie's aunt's legs.

3   Maggie's brother's head is in the same picture as her aunt's body.

4   Maggie's grandpa's legs are now attached to her mother's body.

		Body					Legs				
		Aunt	Brother	Father	Grandpa	Mother	Aunt	Brother	Father	Grandpa	Mother
Head	Aunt										
	Brother										
	Father										
	Grandpa										
	Mother										
Legs	Aunt										
	Brother										
	Father										
	Grandpa										
	Mother										

Head	Body	Legs

Table Talk

Five friends are seated at a table (see diagram below), discussing their favourite hobbies, none of which begins with the same letter as that of his or her name. Find out where they're all sitting, as well as what they like to do in their spare time. (NB – Reference in the clues to 'directly opposite' means as seat A is to seat D, or seat E is to seat B.)

1   The person whose favourite pastime is cooking has a name which begins with the same letter as that of the hobby enjoyed by Walter, who is sitting directly next to Paul.

2   Paul is sitting directly opposite Carol, whose hobby starts with the same letter as that of the name of someone she is sitting next to.

3   The person in seat A isn't Rhona, whose hobby is painting. The person in seat E enjoys walking.

	Carol	Gordon	Paul	Rhona	Walter	Cooking	Gardening	Painting	Reading	Walking
Seat A										
Seat B										
Seat C										
Seat D										
Seat E										
Cooking										
Gardening										
Painting										
Reading										
Walking										

A   B   C

D   E

Seat	Name	Hobby

Families

Each of the four families in this puzzle is made up of a husband, wife, son and daughter, whose names begin with four different letters of the alphabet. Can you decide who is related to whom?

1 Freddie's sister and Clive's wife both have names that start with the same letter.

2 Camilla's brother and Irwin's mother both have names that start with the same letter.

		Wife				Son				Daughter			
		Cathy	Fran	Ingrid	Polly	Colin	Freddie	Irwin	Paul	Camilla	Fern	Isla	Patricia
Husband	Clive												
	Frank												
	Ian												
	Peter												
Daughter	Camilla												
	Fern												
	Isla												
	Patricia												
Son	Colin												
	Freddie												
	Irwin												
	Paul												

Husband	Wife	Son	Daughter

Classroom Competitors

Four girls in the same class at Swotmore High School are very competitive. Last week each came top of the class in one subject and second in another. Use the clues to determine each girl's full name and the two subjects in which she came first and second.

1   The subject in which Erica came first is the same as that in which Miss Cole came second.

2   Jade (whose surname isn't Cole) came second in geography.

3   Miss Sampson came top of the class in history and second in the subject in which Sue came first.

4   Sue didn't come second in English and her surname isn't Morris.

5   The girl who came first in English also came second in mathematics.

6   Lucy (who wasn't top of the class in geography) didn't come second in mathematics.

	Surname				First				Second			
	Brown	Cole	Morris	Sampson	English	Geography	History	Mathematics	English	Geography	History	Mathematics
Erica												
Jade												
Lucy												
Sue												
Second English												
Second Geography												
Second History												
Second Mathematics												
First English												
First Geography												
First History												
First Mathematics												

Girl	Surname	First	Second

Airport Delays

Five people whose flights have been delayed are sitting together in the airport lounge, talking to one another. To which country will each be travelling (eventually!) and for how long has his or her flight been postponed?

1 The passenger travelling to Turkey has a flight delay of four hours.

2 Roger's flight is delayed for a shorter time than that of the traveller bound for Australia, but longer than that of the person (not Marilyn) who is going to Portugal.

3 Eve's flight is delayed for one hour longer than that of the person sitting next to her, who is travelling to Finland.

4 The person flying to Portugal isn't Keith, who is facing a delay two hours shorter than that of Alan's flight.

	Australia	Finland	Japan	Portugal	Turkey	1	2	4	5	6
	Country					**Delay (hours)**				
Alan										
Eve										
Keith										
Marilyn										
Roger										
1 hour										
2 hours										
4 hours										
5 hours										
6 hours										

Traveller	Country	Delay

Bathing Belle

Belle enjoys soaking in the bath. Each evening she chooses a different bath oil to add to the water and, when she's dry, dusts herself with one of five favourite talcum powders. Can you determine which she used on the five listed evenings last week?

1 The apricot bath oil and rose talcum powder were used on different evenings.

2 The magnolia bath oil wasn't chosen by Belle on Monday, although she did use it earlier in the week than the evening on which she dusted herself with lavender talcum powder.

3 The lily bath oil and rose talcum powder were used on two different, non-consecutive evenings. The lily bath oil wasn't used on the same evening as the wisteria talcum powder, and the rose talcum powder wasn't used on the same evening as the strawberry bath oil.

4 The strawberry bath oil, apricot bath oil, wisteria talcum powder and lilac talcum powder were used on different evenings.

	Bath oil					Talc				
	Almond	Apricot	Lily	Magnolia	Strawberry	Lavender	Lilac	Rose	Violet	Wisteria
Monday										
Tuesday										
Wednesday										
Thursday										
Friday										
Lavender					
Lilac					
Rose					
Violet					
Wisteria					

5 Belle used almond bath oil the evening before violet talcum powder, but the evening after she bathed in apricot bath oil.

Evening	Bath oil	Talc

Cross-Stitchers

Four women regularly get together for coffee, a chat and session of cross-stitching. Can you discover each woman's full name, what picture she is working on and how long it has taken her so far?

1   Naomi has been working on her picture for longer than Holly, who isn't cross-stitching a picture of a cat.

2   Shelley is stitching a picture of a mother dog and six puppies. She has been working on her piece for longer than Mrs White.

3   Miss Roper has been working for three hours less time than Grace.

4   The woman sewing a scene of horses in a meadow has been working for one hour less than Mrs Grove, who is stitching a picture of a bowl of flowers.

	Surname				Picture				Hours			
	Grove	Maloney	Roper	White	Cat	Dogs	Flowers	Horses	2	3	5	6
Grace												
Holly												
Naomi												
Shelley												
2 hours												
3 hours												
5 hours												
6 hours												
Cat												
Dogs												
Flowers												
Horses												

Woman	Surname	Picture	Hours

A Moving Story

The four couples in this puzzle are all moving house today. Each is moving from and to two different towns, so can you find out who is married to whom, as well as the name of the towns they are moving from and to?

1 Laura and her husband are moving to the town that Ian and his wife are moving from.

2 Jack and his wife are moving to the town that Laura and her husband are moving from.

3 One of the couples is moving from Broadfield to Dinsdale: Geoff is neither moving from nor to either of these two towns.

4 Hal is married to Katy: they are moving from the town that Naomi and her husband are moving to today.

5 Molly and her husband aren't moving to Applewood.

		Wife				From				To			
		Katy	Laura	Molly	Naomi	Applewood	Broadfield	Cliff Point	Dinsdale	Applewood	Broadfield	Cliff Point	Dinsdale
	Geoff												
	Hal												
	Ian												
	Jack												
To	Applewood												
	Broadfield												
	Cliff Point												
	Dinsdale												
From	Applewood												
	Broadfield												
	Cliff Point												
	Dinsdale												

Husband	Wife	From	To

Five women each received one birthday gift she didn't want, so she wrapped it up again and gave it to a friend (one of the other four women) as a Christmas present – and the recipient was highly pleased to receive it! Who gave to whom, and what was the gift originally received as a birthday present in each case?

1 Abigail received a pair of slippers for Christmas.

2 Brenda gave away an unwanted bottle of perfume, but didn't receive a clock in return.

3 The woman who gave a watch received a book for Christmas.

4 Harriet received a present from Georgina, who didn't receive a present from Brenda.

5 Fern didn't give a Christmas present to Brenda.

	Recipient					Birthday gift				
	Abigail	Brenda	Fern	Georgina	Harriet	Book	Clock	Perfume	Slippers	Watch
Donor Abigail										
Brenda										
Fern										
Georgina										
Harriet										
Birthday gift Book					
Clock					
Perfume					
Slippers					
Watch					

Donor	Recipient	Gift

Oranges and Lemons

Five identical baskets each contain a quantity of oranges and lemons. You can't see them, so you'll need the clues in order to discover how many of each type of fruit are in every basket.

1   No two or more baskets contain exactly the same total number of oranges plus lemons.

2   Basket C contains four fewer lemons than basket E.

3   Basket D contains six more oranges than lemons.

4   Basket A contains twice as many oranges as lemons.

	Oranges					Lemons				
	6	8	10	12	14	6	8	10	12	14
Basket A										
Basket B										
Basket C										
Basket D										
Basket E										

Lemons
6					
8					
10					
12					
14					

Basket	Oranges	Lemons

Car Trouble

It wasn't too long after Mr and Mrs Driver started on a long journey to visit friends that their four children started to complain. How old is each child, what was his or her problem and after travelling what distance did he or she make it known to their long-suffering parents?

1 The youngest child managed to remain 'complaint free' for twice the distance from home than the child who complained of being too cold.

2 Laura started to cry because she was bored with the trip: this began after travelling two kilometres further than the point at which the seven-year-old started to complain.

3 Laura is two years younger than Roy, who managed to remain (relatively) quiet for four kilometres further into the trip than his brother Adam, who didn't moan about being too hot.

	Age				Problem				Distance (km)			
	5	6	7	8	Bored	Car sick	Too cold	Too hot	4	6	8	12
Adam												
Gillian												
Laura												
Roy												
4 kilometres												
6 kilometres												
8 kilometres												
12 kilometres												
Bored												
Car sick												
Too cold												
Too hot												

Child	Age	Problem	Distance

Close Relatives

Four sisters live in neighbouring houses, as you see on the map below. Each is of a different age and has a different number of children. Study the clues to see if you can work out the details and discover where each sister lives.

No 2   No 3   No 4   No 5

1   No woman lives in a house with a number the same as that of the number of children she has.

2   Abigail has one more child than her youngest sister, whose house has a number one higher than that which is home to Fran and her family.

3   Fran is one year older than Glenda, whose house has a number two higher than that which is home to Denise.

4   Abigail's house is somewhere between that of the woman aged 34 and that which is home to Denise (who hasn't four children).

	Sister				Age				Children			
	Abigail	Denise	Fran	Glenda	33	34	35	36	2	3	4	5
No 2												
No 3												
No 4												
No 5												
2 children												
3 children												
4 children												
5 children												
33												
34												
35												
36												

House	Sister	Age	Children

Late Night Line-Up

Provided they were undressed and ready for bed, five children were told they could stay up late to watch a movie on TV. Of course, the children showed an unusual turn of speed! Every child is now seated on the sofa as depicted in the diagram below, but can you speed through these clues to find out the name of the child in each position, as well as the pattern on his or her pyjamas?

1   Of the two boys, one is sitting is position A and the other is wearing pyjamas with a pattern of zigzag lines and is sitting directly next to the girl wearing striped pyjamas.

2   Of Jemima and the girl with large red circles on her pyjamas, one is sitting in position E and the other is sitting directly next to and right of the child whose pyjamas have a pattern of sleepy-looking teddy bears.

3   Of the child in position B and Jodie, one is sitting next to and left of Jimmy and the other is wearing pyjamas patterned with flowers.

4   Jade isn't sitting directly next to Jason or Jodie.

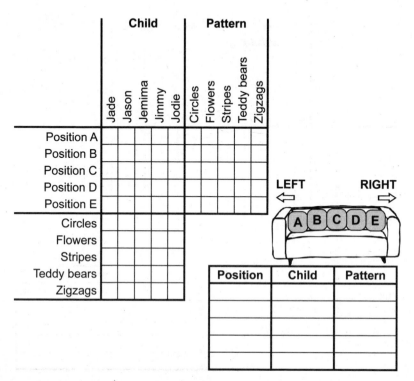

Car Sales

Dave is a secondhand car salesman. Five of his cars have just been reduced in price, having been in his showroom for many months without much interest being shown by buyers, who are unfamiliar with their makes. Can you discover how long Dave has had each car, as well as the very low price at which each is advertised, in the hope that he can get rid of them to make way for more popular vehicles?

1 The green Alvaro isn't priced at $140.

2 The car which Dave has been trying to sell for five months isn't the Mohotsu, which is for sale at a lower price than the Prioto.

3 The Scarba has a price ten dollars lower than that of the Diwitson, which Dave has been trying to sell for longer than the most expensive of the five cars.

4 The Alvaro has been in the showroom for two months longer than the cheapest car, but for less time than the Scarba.

	Time (months)					Price				
	5	6	7	8	9	$110	$120	$130	$140	$150
Alvaro										
Diwitson										
Mohotsu										
Prioto										
Scarba										
$110										
$120										
$130										
$140										
$150										

Make	Time	Price

Keyboard Conundrum

Each of the four women in this puzzle has spent the morning speedily tapping at her computer keyboard responding to various emails from businesses, family members and friends. How many did each woman type?

1 The woman who typed five emails to members of her family sent one more email to friends than Gayle.

2 Gayle emailed one more business than Mandy, who emailed one fewer friend than Zara, who sent fewer emails to her family than were sent by Mandy.

3 The woman (not Zara) who typed two emails to members of her family sent as many emails to friends as Zara sent to members of her family.

4 Zara sent more business emails than the woman who typed the highest number of emails to family members.

		Business				Family				Friends			
		4	6	7	8	2	5	6	9	3	4	6	7
Gayle													
Mandy													
Rose													
Zara													
Friends	3												
	4												
	6												
	7												
Family	2												
	5												
	6												
	9												

Woman	Business	Family	Friends

Combination Numbers

Each of these four people owns a small safe, with a three-digit combination lock. See if you can be a safe-breaker! Just work out the numbers to each person's lock ...

1 Every combination number consists of three different digits.
2 Fred's first digit is higher than his second or his third digit.
3 Mitch's first digit is higher than Pamela's first digit.
4 Mitch's third digit is one lower than Cathy's third digit, which is lower than her first digit.
5 Cathy's second digit isn't one lower than her third digit.

		First				Second				Third			
		2	3	4	5	2	3	4	5	2	3	4	5
	Cathy												
	Fred												
	Mitch												
	Pamela												
Third	2												
Third	3												
Third	4												
Third	5												
Second	2												
Second	3												
Second	4												
Second	5												

Owner	First	Second	Third

Colourful Candles

Candice has five candles of different heights and colours lined up on a shelf, as you see in the diagram below. In the diagram, however, all of the candles are shown as being of the same height (otherwise you wouldn't need any clues in order to tell how tall they are!). Can you work out which is which?

1   The pink candle is further right than the one which is seven centimetres tall, which is next to and left of the green candle.

2   Candle B is one centimetre shorter than the red candle, which is further right than the tallest candle.

3   The white candle is three centimetres shorter than Candice's favourite candle, which is further left than the orange candle.

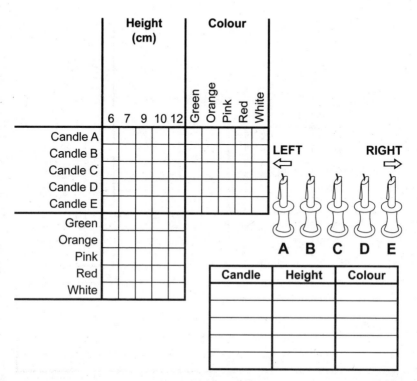

Car Conundrum

Five neighbours live in the houses shown on the map below. Each drives a car of a different colour, so journey through the clues to see if you can discover not only the name of the occupant of each house, but also the colour of his or her vehicle.

1   Rick lives further north and further east than Stella.

2   The person who drives a red car lives next to and north of the owner of the green car, whose house has a number one higher than that belonging to Marie.

3   Leo lives next to and north of the person who drives the blue car, who lives directly east of the owner of the silver car.

		Name					Car				
		Leo	Marie	Pauline	Rick	Stella	Black	Blue	Green	Red	Silver
	No 1										
	No 2										
	No 3										
	No 4										
	No 5										
Car	Black										
	Blue										
	Green										
	Red										
	Silver										

N
W E
S

1
2   3
4   5

House No	Name	Car

Split Personalities

Naughty Nigel has taken photographs of four of his aunts and uncles, cutting each into four pieces (head, body, legs and feet) and then reassembling them in such a way that each 'new' picture contains pieces of four 'old' ones. How have the pictures been reassembled?

1 Aunt Betty's feet are attached to the legs of a man.
2 Uncle Stan's head is attached to Uncle Kevin's body.
3 Uncle Kevin's head and Aunt Helen's legs are in two different pictures.

		Body				Legs				Feet			
		Aunt Betty	Aunt Helen	Uncle Kevin	Uncle Stan	Aunt Betty	Aunt Helen	Uncle Kevin	Uncle Stan	Aunt Betty	Aunt Helen	Uncle Kevin	Uncle Stan
Head	Aunt Betty												
Head	Aunt Helen												
Head	Uncle Kevin												
Head	Uncle Stan												
Feet	Aunt Betty												
Feet	Aunt Helen												
Feet	Uncle Kevin												
Feet	Uncle Stan												
Legs	Aunt Betty												
Legs	Aunt Helen												
Legs	Uncle Kevin												
Legs	Uncle Stan												

Head	Body	Legs	Feet

Playing Cards

The women in this puzzle are playing a game of cards and each has three in her hand: one club, one diamond and one spade. Can you discover which three cards are in each woman's hand? (NB – A=ace, J=jack, Q=queen and K=king; and in the game ace=1, jack=11, queen=12, king=13 and the values of the other cards are as per their numbers.)

1 Sarah's diamond has a value two lower than that of Katy's club, which has a value six higher than that of Lou's spade.

2 The woman with the ace of spades (but not the jack of diamonds) is holding a club with a value two higher than that of Katy's spade, which has a lower value than that of Anna's diamond.

3 The woman with the seven of spades is holding a diamond with a lower value than that of Lou's diamond.

4 Lou's club hasn't a value two higher than that of Anna's diamond.

		Club				Diamond				Spade			
		6	9	10	K	5	7	8	J	A	4	7	Q
	Anna												
	Katy												
	Lou												
	Sarah												
Spade	A												
	4												
	7												
	Q												
Diamond	5												
	7												
	8												
	J												

Player	Club	Diamond	Spade

Towards the end of the academic year, five students met with Professor Crammer, their personal mentor, to discuss their progress at college. At what time was each student's appointment with Professor Crammer, and what was his overall assessment of their work to date?

1 Jack's appointment with Professor Crammer was three quarters of an hour earlier than that of the student who was not very surprised to learn that his progress was 'shameful', since he had not completed a single assignment that year.

2 Kevin was slightly late for his appointment (scheduled for a time one hour later than that of the student assessed as 'steady'), so Professor Crammer felt justified in his assessment of Kevin's progress as 'slow'.

3 The student thought to have made 'superb' progress during the year was seen by Professor Crammer half an hour earlier than the time of George's appointment.

4 Henry's appointment with Professor Crammer was later than half past ten.

	Time					Assessment				
	9.45am	10.00am	10.30am	10.45am	11.00am	Shameful	Slapdash	Slow	Steady	Superb
George										
Henry										
Ivor										
Jack										
Kevin										
Shameful										
Slapdash										
Slow										
Steady										
Superb										

Student	Time	Assessment

Buttons and Bows

Five girls are at the age where they are very much attracted to pretty buttons and bows. Each has collected quite a number, and locks them away in her jewellery box! Can you discover how many buttons and bows have been collected by each girl?

1   Tracey has more bows than the girl with fewest buttons.

2   The girl with the highest number of buttons has 11 fewer bows than Fran, who has either six or 11 fewer buttons than Linda.

3   Amy has 11 fewer buttons than the girl with 15 bows, but Amy has more buttons than Moira, who has more bows than Amy.

	Buttons					Bows				
	7	13	18	24	29	4	9	15	21	26
Amy										
Fran										
Linda										
Moira										
Tracey										
4										
9										
15										
21										
26										

Bows

Girl	Buttons	Bows

In Tents Study

At the annual International Girl Guides Camp, eight girls from different Canadian cities decided to pitch their tents next to one another. In every tent, there were two girls from the same city, who shared a tent with one another, since they knew each other well and were in the same group at home. Can you discover which tent each pair shared, as well as their home city? A plan of the tents is laid out below.

1   Adele and Colette were in tents separated from each other by at least one other tent. Adele's tent was next to and left of that shared by the Guides from Vancouver.

2   Victoria was in a tent next to and left of that occupied by Nicole.

3   The girls from Toronto (who weren't in tent C) both got on well with Jessica, whose tent was next to and right of that shared by the Guides from Ottawa.

4   Tracey and Olivia shared a tent further right than (but not directly next to) that shared by Laura and her friend.

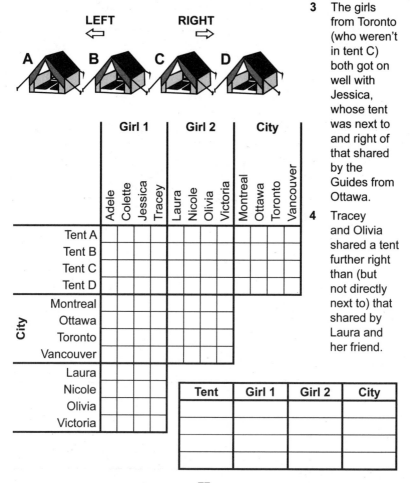

LEFT ⇦   **RIGHT** ⇨

A   B   C   D

	Girl 1				Girl 2				City			
	Adele	Colette	Jessica	Tracey	Laura	Nicole	Olivia	Victoria	Montreal	Ottawa	Toronto	Vancouver
Tent A												
Tent B												
Tent C												
Tent D												
Montreal								
Ottawa								
Toronto								
Vancouver								
Laura				
Nicole				
Olivia				
Victoria				

City (row label on left)

Tent	Girl 1	Girl 2	City

73 Birthday Celebrations

Four couples celebrated birthdays on various days last week. Use the clues to discover the birthdays of each couple.

1 Ben's birthday was the day before that of Tina's husband.

2 Jamie's wife's birthday fell the day after Rodney's birthday; and Rodney's wife's birthday fell the day after Jamie's birthday!

3 Sarah's husband's birthday was the day after Louise's birthday.

4 Ben's wife's birthday fell either two or three days after Tina's birthday.

5 Sarah's birthday was more than one day earlier in the week than that of Jamie's wife.

	Wife				His birthday				Her birthday			
	Cora	Louise	Sarah	Tina	Monday	Wednesday	Thursday	Friday	Monday	Tuesday	Thursday	Friday
Ben												
Jamie												
Rodney												
Vince												
Hers Monday												
Hers Tuesday												
Hers Thursday												
Hers Friday												
His Monday												
His Wednesday												
His Thursday												
His Friday												

Husband	Wife	His	Hers

At the Bus Stop

After a morning spent shopping in town, five women are waiting for a bus to take them home. From the clues and the diagram below, can you identify each woman and the colour of her shopping bag?

1 The five women are: the woman who is fourth in the queue; Cindy; the woman with the black shopping bag; the woman who is last in the queue; and Joan.

2 The five women are: Maureen; the woman who is first in the queue; the woman (not Vera) with the brown shopping bag; Thelma; and the woman with the green shopping bag.

3 The five women are: the woman who is fifth in the queue; Joan; the woman standing directly in front of Joan; the woman with the brown shopping bag; and Maureen (who isn't carrying a blue shopping bag).

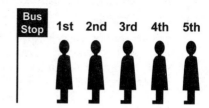

	Cindy	Joan	Maureen	Thelma	Vera	Black	Blue	Brown	Green	Red
First										
Second										
Third										
Fourth										
Fifth										
Black										
Blue										
Brown										
Green										
Red										

Position	Name	Bag

Business Trips

During the final two months of the year, the five people in this puzzle made business trips abroad, each visiting two different countries. Everyone made one trip in November and one in December and no two people visited the same country in either month. Where did they all go?

1 If Kevin went to Portugal in December, then Jill went to Egypt in November; otherwise Jill went to Portugal in December.

2 If whoever went to Venezuela in November also went to Brazil in December, then Lucy went to Greece in December; otherwise whoever went to Venezuela in November also went to Egypt in December and Lucy went to Greece in November.

3 If Brian went to Brazil in November, then Arthur went to Venezuela in December; otherwise Brian went to Brazil in December and Arthur went to Egypt in November (as well as to either Venezuela or Greece in December).

4 If Kevin went to Egypt in November, then Lucy went to Brazil in November; otherwise Kevin went to Greece in November.

	November					December				
	Brazil	Egypt	Greece	Portugal	Venezuela	Brazil	Egypt	Greece	Portugal	Venezuela
Arthur										
Brian										
Jill										
Kevin										
Lucy										
Brazil (December)										
Egypt (December)										
Greece (December)										
Portugal (December)										
Venezuela (December)										

Name	November	December

Postal Service

Shortly after the postal counter opened this morning, four people could be seen queueing to buy stamps and one other item. Can you determine each person's position in the queue, together with the number of stamps and other item he or she purchased?

1 The person buying a ruler was standing directly in front of Marilyn, who wanted two more stamps than the person who was first in the queue.

2 There was one person between Liz and the customer who was buying a pencil.

3 The customer who wanted fewest stamps was directly in front of the one who was buying a notebook, who didn't want one fewer stamp than the person who was last in the queue.

4 Toby (who wanted to buy an eraser) was two places ahead of Zach in the queue.

	Position				Stamps				Other			
	First	Second	Third	Fourth	4	5	6	8	Eraser	Notebook	Pencil	Ruler
Liz												
Marilyn												
Toby												
Zach												
Eraser								
Notebook								
Pencil								
Ruler								
4 stamps				
5 stamps				
6 stamps				
8 stamps				

Name	Position	Stamps	Other

Happy Birthday

Four friends each have a birthday on a different day next week. Can you work out each child's surname, the day on which his or her birthday falls, and each child's age?

1 Ben is two years older than the child whose birthday is two days after Ben's.

2 The child surnamed Grove has a birthday two days before Stephen's.

3 Stephen is one year older than the child surnamed Jackson, whose birthday is the day before Joanne's.

4 Alice's birthday is either the day before or the day after that of the boy surnamed Hibbert.

	Surname				Birthday				Age			
	Grove	Hibbert	Ivy	Jackson	Tuesday	Wednesday	Thursday	Saturday	5	7	8	9
Alice												
Ben												
Joanne												
Stephen												
Age 5												
7												
8												
9												
Birthday Tuesday												
Wednesday												
Thursday												
Saturday												

Child	Surname	Birthday	Age

Crocuses and Snowdrops

Five children have each planted a pot of bulbs, which will flower in the spring and bring cheer to all that see them. How many crocuses and snowdrops did each child plant?

1 Laura planted more snowdrops than Norman, but fewer than Michael.
2 Katie planted more crocuses than Norman, but fewer than Michael.
3 The child who planted the highest number of crocuses also planted four more snowdrops than Katie.
4 Laura planted exactly the same number of crocuses as the number of snowdrops planted by Joe.

	Crocuses					Snowdrops				
	9	10	13	14	15	10	14	16	20	22
Joe										
Katie										
Laura										
Michael										
Norman										
Snowdrops 10					
14					
16					
20					
22					

Child	Crocuses	Snowdrops

83

Easter Eggs

Last Easter, Karen was given five chocolate Easter eggs, each wrapped in foil of a different colour to the others. Who gave each egg and in what order did Karen eat them all?

1   Doug didn't give the Easter egg wrapped in blue foil, which Karen ate directly after eating the egg she consumed directly after eating the egg wrapped in gold foil, which was a gift from Cheryl.

2   The Easter egg from Doug was eaten later than the one in silver foil which, in turn, was eaten later than the one in pink foil.

3   The Easter egg given to Karen by Benny was eaten directly after that wrapped in purple foil, which wasn't eaten directly after the egg that was consumed directly after the egg given by Stella.

	Benny	Cheryl	Doug	Larry	Stella	First	Second	Third	Fourth	Fifth
Blue										
Gold										
Pink										
Purple										
Silver										
First										
Second										
Third										
Fourth										
Fifth										

Foil	Given by	Order

Quiz Night Challenge

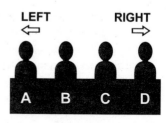

It's Quiz Night at the local sports club and thirty teams, each of four people, are taking part. This puzzle concerns just one of those teams, and your challenge is to discover the full name of each person at their table (see plan below), together with the subject about which each individual is most knowledgeable.

1 Donald is further left than the science expert, who is sitting next to and between Vanessa and the person surnamed Wallis.

2 Elizabeth is sitting next to and between the person surnamed Porter and the one whose specialist subject is music.

3 Elizabeth isn't the person knowledgeable about politics (who is seated further right than Vanessa) nor is Elizabeth sitting next to the person whose specialist subject is politics.

4 Donald isn't sitting next to and left of the person surnamed Scott.

		Name				Surname				Subject			
		Donald	Elizabeth	Jason	Vanessa	Castle	Porter	Scott	Wallis	Music	Politics	Science	Sport
	Person A												
	Person B												
	Person C												
	Person D												
Subject	Music												
	Politics												
	Science												
	Sport												
Surname	Castle												
	Porter												
	Scott												
	Wallis												

Person	Name	Surname	Subject

Nature Table

Four children each brought some berries, flowers and leaves to school today, to place on the classroom nature table, so that their teacher could talk about them to the class, after which the children made a collage and displayed it on the wall. Can you discover how many berries, flowers and leaves each child brought to school? (NB – Each child brought three different quantities of all three items.)

1   Andrew brought the same number of leaves as the number of berries brought by the child who brought five flowers.

2   Cheryl brought the same number of flowers as the number of leaves brought by the child who brought seven berries.

3   Darren brought one more leaf than the child who brought nine flowers, but one fewer leaf than the child who brought five berries.

		Berries				Flowers				Leaves			
		4	5	6	7	5	6	7	9	4	6	7	8
	Andrew												
	Cheryl												
	Darren												
	Emily												
Leaves	4												
	6												
	7												
	8												
Flowers	5												
	6												
	7												
	9												

Child	Berries	Flowers	Leaves

Home Improvement

Five people who moved into old properties undertook two major improvement projects last year, entirely redecorating and modernizing their bathrooms and kitchens. Can you work out the two different months in which each carried out the works?

1. If Deirdre decorated her bathroom in July, then Samuel decorated his kitchen in August; otherwise Deirdre decorated her bathroom in May, and Lola decorated her kitchen in August.

2. If Deirdre did her kitchen in July, then Nigel updated his bathroom in May; otherwise Nigel updated his bathroom in the same month as Samuel did his kitchen, and two months before Lola's kitchen project.

3. If the person who modernized a bathroom in March also decorated a kitchen in August, then Graeme decorated his bathroom in September; otherwise the person who modernized a bathroom in March also decorated a kitchen in April, and Graeme decorated his kitchen in August.

4. If Lola modernized her bathroom in March, then Nigel decorated his kitchen in April; otherwise Lola modernized her bathroom in September and Nigel decorated his bathroom in May.

	Bathroom					Kitchen				
	March	May	June	July	September	April	June	July	August	October
Deirdre										
Graeme										
Lola										
Nigel										
Samuel										
Kitchen April					
June					
July					
August					
October					

Name	Bathroom	Kitchen

Soap Operas

Chris loves watching soap operas on television; which is just as well, since there are so many at the moment. His five favourites are broadcast twice a week, so view the clues below to discover on which two nights each two episodes are shown. (NB – The soaps are shown on different nights, the first episode of each being broadcast earlier in the week than the second episode.)

1 The soap shown first on Tuesday has its second episode broadcast on Sunday evenings.

2 The first and second episodes of *Driftwood* are both broadcast earlier in the week than the first and second episodes of *Hospital Life* (one episode of which is shown on the same night as one of the episodes of *The Saga*).

3 The second episode of *The Saga* is broadcast earlier in the week than the first episode of *Hobart Hill*.

	First					Second				
	Monday	Tuesday	Wednesday	Thursday	Friday	Wednesday	Thursday	Friday	Saturday	Sunday
Driftwood										
Family Feud										
Hobart Hill										
Hospital Life										
The Saga										
Second Wednesday					
Thursday					
Friday					
Saturday					
Sunday					

Soap	First	Second

Brick Stack

The picture below shows four bricks, placed one on top of the other. On every brick, there is a number on one side and a picture of an animal on another of the six sides. You can't see these, of course, so you'll need the clues to determine what is on each brick, as well as its colour.

1 The orange brick is directly on top of that with a picture of a leopard, but directly next to and below that on which the number 7 has been printed.

2 The number on the pink brick is two higher than that on the one with a picture of an Arctic fox, which is directly on top of the brick with a 2 printed on one of its six sides, which is higher in the stack than the pink brick.

3 The number printed on the brick with a picture of an elephant is lower than the number on the brown brick, which isn't directly on top of nor directly next to and below the turquoise brick.

	Number				Animal				Colour			
	2	3	5	7	Elephant	Fox	Iguana	Leopard	Brown	Orange	Pink	Turquoise
Brick A												
Brick B												
Brick C												
Brick D												
Brown												
Orange												
Pink												
Turquoise												
Elephant												
Fox												
Iguana												
Leopard												

A

B

C

D

Brick	Number	Animal	Colour

Babysitters

Four sisters regularly babysit for neighbours, in order to raise some pocket money. What is the name of the child each girl looks after, what is his or her age and on which evening of the week does each sister look after him or her?

1 The child looked after by Barbara is older than David, for whose parents one of the sisters babysits the evening after Faith takes care of a child.

2 The child looked after by Jeanne is older than Sheila's charge, for whose parents Sheila babysits two evenings later than the babysitting evening of the girl (not Jeanne) who takes care of Teresa.

3 Louella is five years old and is looked after earlier in the week than Jeanne's babysitting evening, but later in the week than that of the sister who looks after the oldest child.

	Child				Age				Evening			
	David	Louella	Patrick	Teresa	3	5	7	8	Tuesday	Wednesday	Thursday	Saturday
Barbara												
Faith												
Jeanne												
Sheila												
Tuesday												
Wednesday												
Thursday												
Saturday												
Age 3												
5												
7												
8												

Sister	Child	Age	Evening

Split Personalities

Tired with her mother's obsession with watching fictional detective movies on TV, Laura has cut pictures of five of her mother's favourite sleuths each into three pieces (head, body and legs), reassembling them in such a way that each 'new' picture contains pieces of three 'old' ones. How have the pictures been reassembled?

1. The legs of Ngaio Marsh's famous detective, Roderick Alleyn, are now attached to the elderly body of Miss Jane Marple, but his body is not attached to her head.

2. The head of Dorothy L Sayers' detective, Lord Peter Wimsey, is in the same picture as the legs of Hercule Poirot.

3. Of the two detectives created by Agatha Christie, Jane Marple and Hercule Poirot, Poirot's body is attached to Miss Marple's legs.

4. Hercule Poirot's head and Roderick Alleyn's legs are in two different pictures.

5. Sherlock Holmes's body is not attached to Lord Peter Wimsey's legs.

		Body					Legs				
		Alleyn	Holmes	Marple	Poirot	Wimsey	Alleyn	Holmes	Marple	Poirot	Wimsey
Head	Alleyn										
	Holmes										
	Marple										
	Poirot										
	Wimsey										
Legs	Alleyn										
	Holmes										
	Marple										
	Poirot										
	Wimsey										

Head	Body	Legs

Round of Drinks

Seated around the table (as drawn in the picture below) are five men, each of whom is drinking something different to the other four. Can you work out who is in each numbered seat, together with his drink?

1   John is seated directly between Colin and the man with a glass of water.

2   The man with a mug of tea is directly next to and clockwise of Kenny.

3   The man with a glass of beer is directly next to and clockwise of Ivan.

4   Harry is directly next to and clockwise of the man drinking tea.

5   The man in seat 1 has a glass of cola. Colin is drinking coffee.

	Name					Drink				
	Colin	Harry	Ivan	John	Kenny	Beer	Coffee	Cola	Tea	Water
Seat 1										
Seat 2										
Seat 3										
Seat 4										
Seat 5										
Beer										
Coffee										
Cola										
Tea										
Water										

Clockwise

Seat	Name	Drink

Wine Lake

Tasked with buying different snacks for the office party, the four women in this puzzle all forgot what they were supposed to get and bought wine instead – so there was rather a lot of it at the party! No woman bought the same number of bottles of either red, rosé or white wine as any other, and each bought three different quantities. Swim through the clues to see if you can determine the facts.

1   Whoever bought the highest number of bottles of rosé also purchased one fewer bottle of white wine than Nadine.

2   Madge didn't buy exactly the same number of bottles of rosé as the number of bottles of white wine purchased by Olivia.

3   Olivia bought one fewer bottle of red wine than the woman who bought the fewest bottles of white wine.

4   Leonie purchased one fewer bottle of white wine than the woman who bought four bottles of red wine.

5   The woman who bought five bottles of white wine also purchased two fewer bottles of rosé than Madge.

	Red (bottles)				Rosé (bottles)				White (bottles)			
	3	4	5	6	3	4	5	6	3	4	5	6
Leonie												
Madge												
Nadine												
Olivia												
White 3												
White 4												
White 5												
White 6												
Rosé 3												
Rosé 4												
Rosé 5												
Rosé 6												

Woman	Red	Rosé	White

The Haunted Manor

Deep in the heart of Wiltshire, England, is an old manor house, said to be haunted. Harry is the guide who conducts tourists around the manor on Ghost Nights, which are held every week during the summer months. Up until the final week of the last summer season, nothing much happened: but on the last four nights, each party heard something unexplained. How many were in each party that Harry escorted, where were they when the noise was heard and what did they hear?

1   The ghostly footsteps weren't heard in the library.

2   The haunting sound of someone whistling at the far end of the ballroom was heard by a smaller party of people than that which Harry conducted around the manor on Wednesday.

3   Monday's party consisted of two fewer people than those who heard a noise in the cellar.

4   Thursday's group heard breaking glass and numbered three more people than those who heard a door banging.

5   The unexplained noise in the kitchen occurred on Tuesday.

	Party				Location				Heard			
	7	9	10	12	Ballroom	Cellar	Kitchen	Library	Breaking glass	Door banging	Footsteps	Whistling
Monday												
Tuesday												
Wednesday												
Thursday												
Breaking glass												
Door banging												
Footsteps												
Whistling												
Ballroom												
Cellar												
Kitchen												
Library												

Night	Party	Location	Heard

Throwing Pots

Caroline makes clay pots, which she sells at a market stall every Saturday. Last week she made various quantities of pots on five different days, painting each day's batch a different colour, after it had been fired in her kiln. How many pots did she make each day, and in what colour?

1 Caroline made three more orange pots than green pots.

2 The green pots were made two days before the blue pots.

3 Caroline made five more blue pots than the number of pots produced on Friday.

4 The brown pots were made earlier in the week than the smallest quantity, but later in the week than the largest quantity.

5 The brown pots weren't made the day before the yellow pots.

	Quantity					Colour				
	6	11	16	19	22	Blue	Brown	Green	Orange	Yellow
Monday										
Tuesday										
Wednesday										
Thursday										
Friday										
Blue					
Brown					
Green					
Orange					
Yellow					

Day	Quantity	Colour

Fruit and Nut Suppers

Colin often feels hungry in the evenings, so needs a snack at about nine o'clock. He chooses something healthy to eat, having a different mixture of fruit and nuts each night. Can you discover what he had for supper on each of five nights last week?

1   The apple was eaten later in the week than the pineapple.

2   The banana was eaten later in the week than both the almonds and brazils, but earlier in the week than the pear.

3   The cashews were eaten earlier in the week than both the banana and the peach, but later in the week than the brazil nuts.

4   The pecans weren't eaten the evening after the almonds.

	Fruit					Nuts				
	Apple	Banana	Peach	Pear	Pineapple	Almonds	Brazils	Cashews	Pecans	Walnuts
Monday										
Tuesday										
Wednesday										
Thursday										
Friday										
Almonds					
Brazils					
Cashews					
Pecans					
Walnuts					

Night	Fruit	Nuts

Playing Cards

The four men in this puzzle are playing a game of cards and each has three in his hand: one heart, one diamond and one spade. Can you discover which three cards are in each man's hand? (NB – A=ace, J=jack, Q=queen and K=king; and in the game, ace=1, jack=11, queen=12, king=13 and the values of the other cards are as per their numbers.)

1   The man with the ten of hearts is holding a diamond with a value one lower than that of the spade which the man with the king of hearts is holding.

2   Mitch's spade has a value two lower than that of the spade held by the man whose diamond has a value two lower than that of Keith's diamond.

3   Keith's spade has a value four lower than that of the heart held by Mitch.

4   One man is holding both the four of spades and the seven of diamonds, together with a heart which has a value two higher than that of the heart held by Neil.

		Heart				Diamond				Spade			
		8	10	J	K	A	3	5	7	4	6	8	Q
	Frank												
	Keith												
	Mitch												
	Neil												
Spade	4												
	6												
	8												
	Q												
Diamond	A												
	3												
	5												
	7												

Player	Heart	Diamond	Spade

No Loose Screws

Eric is fond of home improvement, especially woodworking, and likes
to be able to find things easily and quickly whenever he's building
something new. Much of his work involves using screws, and all the
different types he needs are stored in the unit you see in the diagram.
How many screws are currently in each of the drawers at the three
different levels (top, middle and bottom)?

1 Drawer A in the bottom level contains four more screws than A in the
   middle level, which holds two fewer screws than D in the top level.
2 The letter identifying the drawer with fewest screws in the top level is
   the same as that of the drawer which holds 22 screws in the middle
   level, but not 34 in the bottom level.
3 The drawer with 32 screws in the middle level is further left than the
   one (not C) with 24 screws in the bottom level.
4 The drawer with 18 screws in the bottom level is directly next to and
   right of a drawer identified by the same letter as the one in the middle
   level which contains two more screws than D in the bottom level.
5 The total number of screws in the three drawers marked C is higher
   than the total number of screws in the three drawers marked A.

Will's Wind-Ups

Will is very bad at remembering to wind up the five clocks in his house, with the result that each of them stopped at a different time on a different day last week. Can you time yourself to see how quickly you can discover the time and day each clock stopped?

1   The carriage clock stopped working at a time three and a quarter hours earlier than the grandfather clock, which stopped two days after the carriage clock, which stopped later in the week than the clock which stopped at 10.15am.

2   The alarm clock stopped working at a time seven hours earlier than a clock which didn't stop at all on Thursday.

3   The wall clock stopped the day after the one which ceased working at 6.30am.

	Time					Day				
	3.15am	6.30am	10.15am	5.15pm	8.30pm	Monday	Wednesday	Thursday	Friday	Sunday
Alarm clock										
Carriage clock										
Cuckoo clock										
Grandfather clock										
Wall clock										
Monday										
Wednesday										
Thursday										
Friday										
Sunday										

Clock	Time	Day

Happy Memories

Pete and Polly recently spent an evening looking at their photograph albums, recalling events from earlier times, when their son Philip was growing up. Can you work out the month and year in which each event took place?

1 The photograph of Philip acting as a pageboy at his cousin's wedding were taken in an earlier year (and in an earlier month of the year) than those of Philip on the day he played the violin in a school concert.

2 Not surprisingly, the pictures connected with Christmas were taken in December! The pictures of Philip's birthday party were taken two years later.

3 The set of pictures taken in 1986 were of an event which took place two months later in the year than those from 1991, but earlier in the year than those taken in 1996.

4 One of the albums contained pictures of a holiday taken in May.

	Month					Year				
	March	May	July	September	December	1986	1989	1991	1994	1996
Birthday										
Christmas										
Concert										
Holiday										
Wedding										
1986					
1989					
1991					
1994					
1996					

Event	Month	Year

Solutions

No 1

The youngest person (aged 28, grid) isn't the artist (clue 1), doctor (clue 2) or baker (3), so the teacher is 28. He/she isn't Katie (1), Martin (2) or John (5), so Penny. Martin lives at No 2 (2). Penny lives at either No 3 or No 4 (3). The person who lives at No 1 isn't John (4), so Katie. She isn't 31 (4), so she's 30 (1), the artist is 29 and the person at No 3 is 28 (Penny, above). By elimination, John lives at No 4. Katie is the baker (3). Martin isn't 31 (2), so he's 29 (artist, above) and John is 31. John is the doctor.

Thus:

No 1 - Katie - 30 - baker;
No 2 - Martin - 29 - artist;
No 3 - Penny - 28 - teacher;
No 4 - John - 31 - doctor.

No 2

Digger the terrier (clue 1) doesn't belong to Mike. Nor is he Joanna's or Louise's dog (clue 2), or David's (3), so Digger belongs to Alan. David's dog is Nero (3). Mike's isn't Bobo (2) or Jinx (5), so Sam. Joanna's isn't Jinx (5), so Bobo. Louise's dog is Jinx, thus (2) Jinx is the Alsatian. The poodle doesn't belong to Mike or David (4), so to Joanna. Sam isn't the spaniel (6), so the collie. David owns the spaniel.

Thus:

Alan - Digger - terrier;
David - Nero - spaniel;
Joanna - Bobo - poodle;
Louise - Jinx - Alsatian;
Mike - Sam - collie.

No 3

Remember throughout that no woman visited on Wednesday (grid). Brenda thus visited on Tuesday (clue 1), the woman with the cake came on Monday, and the one who visited on Thursday brought a magazine. Alice came on Saturday (clue 3), so Mary's visit was on Thursday (2), the honey was brought on Tuesday, and Sharon visited on Monday. Doreen visited on Friday. The book wasn't from Alice (3), so Doreen. Alice gave fruit.

Thus:

Monday - Sharon - cake;
Tuesday - Brenda - honey;
Thursday - Mary - magazine;
Friday - Doreen book;
Saturday - Alice - fruit.

No 4

Lesley has lessons on either Wednesday or Thursday (clue 1), as does Sally (clue 2), so Hope has lessons on Tuesday (3) and Des has lessons on Monday, with (by elimination) Thelma. They're learning the quickstep (2) and Sally's lessons are on Wednesday. Thus Lesley's lessons are on Thursday. Lesley isn't learning the foxtrot or the waltz (1), so the tango with (4) Ray. Cliff's foxtrot lessons (1) are on Wednesday, so John's are on Tuesday (with Hope, above). Cliff's partner is Sally.

Thus:

Cliff - Sally - Wednesday - foxtrot;
Des - Thelma - Monday - quickstep;
John - Hope - Tuesday - waltz;
Ray - Lesley - Thursday - tango.

Solutions

No 5

Friday's movie wasn't the western (clue 1) thriller or romance (clue 2), so the sci-fi movie. Thursday's wasn't the western (1) or romance (2), so the thriller. Thus Hal went to the cinema on Friday (2) the romance was on Wednesday, and the western was on Tuesday. Sam and Kathryn went on Wednesday (1) and Julia went on Thursday. Lorna went on Tuesday (3) and Mike went on Thursday. Thus Lester went on Tuesday and Meryl went on Friday.

Thus:

Tuesday - Lester - Lorna - western;
Wednesday - Sam - Kathryn - romance;
Thursday - Mike - Julia - thriller;
Friday - Hal - Meryl - sci-fi.

No 6

Henry captained the hockey team (clue 2) and Dean captained the swimming club (clue 3). Peter, who was a captain in 2003, didn't captain the baseball or archery teams (4), so he was captain of the badminton team. Thus the man who led the archery team was captain in 2001 (1). He isn't Frank (3), so Joe. Frank led the baseball team. Henry was a captain in 2002 (2), so Dean was a captain in 2004 (3) and Frank in 2005.

Thus:

Dean - swimming - 2004;
Frank - baseball - 2005;
Henry - hockey - 2002;
Joe - archery - 2001;
Peter - badminton - 2003.

No 7

Parcel A isn't from Aunt Debbie (clue 1), Uncle Jim (clue 2), Aunt Lily (3) or Aunt Ann (4), so Uncle Pete. It isn't the wristwatch (3), so B isn't from Aunt Lily. A doesn't contain a book (1), so B isn't from Aunt Debbie. Nor is B from Uncle Jim (2), so B is from Aunt Ann and (4) contains make-up. C isn't from Aunt Debbie (1) or Aunt Lily (3), so Uncle Jim. E doesn't contain a book (1), wristwatch (3) or purse (4), so a clock. By elimination, A contains a purse. D isn't from Aunt Lily (3), so Aunt Debbie. E is from Aunt Lily. C contains a book (1), so the wristwatch is in D.

Thus:

Parcel A - purse - Uncle Peter;
Parcel B - make-up - Aunt Ann;
Parcel C - book - Uncle Jim;
Parcel D - wristwatch - Aunt Debbie;
Parcel E - clock - Aunt Lily.

No 8

The interview with Dora Dean is at either 10.00am or 11.00am (clue 3), as is that with Ed Evans (clue 4), so Frank Fair's interview is at 2.00pm (1) and the dancer's is at 3.00pm. Frank Fair is the footballer (3). By elimination, Gina Gold's interview is at 3.00pm. She will be seen on Wednesday (2). Frank Fair's interview is thus on Friday (3) and Dora Dean's is on Thursday. Ed Evans will be interviewed on Tuesday. He isn't a singer (4), so a writer. Dora Dean is thus the singer, so her interview is at 11.00am (4) and the 10.00am interview is with Ed Evans.

Solutions

Thus:

Dora Dean - Thursday - 11.00am - singer;

Ed Evans - Tuesday - 10.00am - writer;

Frank Fair - Friday - 2.00pm - footballer;

Gina Gold - Wednesday - 3.00pm - dancer.

No 9

Remember throughout that each new picture is made of pieces of four old ones (intro). Mrs Nuffin's feet and Miss Fortune's head (clue 2) are in the same picture. They're not with Mr Trick's legs (clue 2), so they're with Miss Givins' legs and (by elimination) Mr Trick's body. Miss Givins' body is in the same picture as Mr Trick's legs (1), so they're with Mrs Nuffin's head and (by elimination) Miss Fortune's feet. By elimination, Mr Trick's feet are with Miss Givins' head; and Miss Givins' feet are with Mr Trick's head. The latter aren't with Mrs Nuffin's legs (3), so they're with Miss Fortune's legs and (by elimination) Mrs Nuffin's body. Miss Givins' head is thus with Miss Fortune's body and Mrs Nuffin's legs.

Thus (head - body - legs - feet):

Miss Fortune - Mr Trick - Miss Givins - Mrs Nuffin;

Miss Givins - Miss Fortune - Mrs Nuffin - Mr Trick;

Mrs Nuffin - Miss Givins - Mr Trick - Miss Fortune;

Mr Trick - Mrs Nuffin - Miss Fortune - Miss Givins.

No 10

Gemma has written 110 words (clue 4). No-one wrote 140 words (grid), so the GIRL (clue 1) who went to India and has written either 90 or 100 words is (by elimination) Bella. Thus Bella has written 100 words (2) and the child who went to Japan has written 90 words. Thus Douglas went to Japan (5) and Gemma went to Antigua. Saul went to Holland (3), and Arnie wrote 130 words (1), so Saul has written 120 words. Arnie went to France.

Thus:

Arnie - 130 words - France;

Bella - 100 words - India;

Douglas - 90 words - Japan;

Gemma - 110 words - Antigua;

Saul - 120 words - Holland.

No 11

The piece made on Tuesday came from a shirt (clue 2). The tail was made from a blouse (clue 1) on either Thursday or Friday. The hind legs were also made on either Thursday or Friday (3), so the forelegs were made on Saturday. The hind legs were made the day after the piece with material from the trousers (3), so the tail made from the blouse was done on Friday, the hind legs were made on Thursday, and the piece with material from the trousers was made on Wednesday. The head was made on Wednesday (1), so the body was made on Tuesday. The forelegs (Saturday, above) were made from the curtain (1), so the hind legs were made of material from the jacket.

Thus:

Tuesday - body - shirt;

Wednesday - head - trousers;

Thursday - hind legs - jacket;

Friday - tail - blouse;

Saturday - forelegs - curtain.

Solutions

No 12

The 4-year-old (youngest) isn't Connor (clue 1), Felix (clue 2) or Martine (3), so Deanna. The 7-year-old isn't Connor (1) or Martine (3), so Felix. His gift isn't the hat (2), so Connor is 5 (1) and the hat is for the 6-year-old, who is thus Martine. Felix's mother is Chrissie (3). He isn't getting mittens (2) or a scarf (3), so a sweater. Deanna's mother is Daphne (1). She isn't getting a scarf (4), so mittens. Connor will get a scarf. Martine's mother isn't Flora (5), so Mary. Connor's is Flora.

Thus (child - mother):
Hat - Martine - Mary - 6 years old;
Mittens - Deanna - Daphne -
    4 years old;
Scarf - Connor - Flora - 5 years old;
Sweater - Felix - Chrissie -
    7 years old.

No 13

Remember throughout that the four members of each family all have names starting with different letters (intro). Barbara's brother isn't Charlie (clue 1) or Andy (clue 3), so Dave. Their mother isn't Angela (4), so Camilla; thus their father is Austin. Angela's son is Charlie (4). Doreen's husband is Clive (2), so (by elimination) Bill's wife is Angela and Brenda's husband is Douglas. Thus Brian's father isn't Douglas, so Clive. Charlie's sister is Dawn (1), so their father is Bill. Andy's father is Douglas and his sister is Clarissa. Alison's father is Clive.

Thus (husband - wife - son - daughter):
Austin - Camilla - Dave - Barbara;
Bill - Angela - Charlie - Dawn;
Clive - Doreen - Brian - Alison;
Douglas - Brenda - Andy - Clarissa.

No 14

Jane hates cabbage (clue 3). The child who loves cabbage isn't Lynda (clue 1), Mark or Carla (2), so Dennis. Jane loves peas (1). Dennis doesn't hate beans or peas (1) or carrots (4), so turnips. Lynda loves turnips (1). The child who hates peas isn't Lynda or Mark (2), so Carla. The child who loves beans and hates carrots (4) is thus Mark. Carla loves carrots. Lynda hates beans.

Thus (loves - hates):
Carla - carrots - peas;
Dennis - cabbage - turnips;
Jane - peas - cabbage;
Lynda - turnips - beans;
Mark - beans - carrots.

No 15

No woman visited at 12.00pm or 1.00pm (grid), so Judith's visit was at either 2.00pm or 3.00pm (clue 1), as was Penny's (clue 2). The 4.00pm visitor wasn't Fran (1) or Eva (3), so Carolyn. The 10.00am visitor wasn't Eva (3), so Fran visited at 10.00am (1) and Judith at 2.00pm. Thus Penny visited at 3.00pm (above), so Eva visited at 11.00am. Carolyn visited on Thursday (2), Fran on Wednesday (3) and Judith on Tuesday (1). Eva didn't visit on Friday (3), so on Saturday. Penny visited on Friday.

Thus:
Tuesday - Judith - 2.00pm;
Wednesday - Fran - 10.00am;
Thursday - Carolyn - 4.00pm;
Friday - Penny - 3.00pm;
Saturday - Eva - 11.00am.

No 16

Karen's surname is Fox (clue 1) and person C is surnamed Grove

Solutions

(clue 4). Barry who is person D (5) isn't surnamed Watson, so O'Brien. Rory's surname isn't Grove (4), so Watson. Thus Maxine is person C (4) surnamed Grove. Person B wants Brie (3). Karen and/or Rory are A and/or B, so Rory isn't the MAN (1) who wants Gouda. Thus Barry wants Gouda, so Karen is person B (1) and Rory is thus person A. Maxine doesn't want Camembert (2), so Edam. Rory wants Camembert.

Thus:

Person A - Rory - Watson - Camembert;
Person B - Karen - Fox - Brie;
Person C - Maxine - Grove - Edam;
Person D - Barry - O'Brien - Gouda.

No 17

The child with 4 (fewest) milk chocolates isn't Pippa (clue 1), Sean or Jasmine (clue 2), so Callum. Pippa has 6 milk chocolates (1), so Sean has 8 (2) and Jasmine has 10. Jasmine has either 8 dark and 7 white (3) or 10 dark and 9 white. So the child with 9 dark chocolates isn't Jasmine. Nor is he/she Pippa or Callum (1), so Sean. Sean has either 7 or 9 white chocolates (2), as has Jasmine (above), so Sean has 7 (1) and Pippa has 5. By elimination, Callum has 3 white chocolates, and Jasmine has 9 white (3) and 10 dark chocolates. Callum hasn't 7 dark chocolates (4), so 8. Pippa has 7 dark chocolates.

Thus (dark - milk - white):

Callum - 8 - 4 - 3;
Jasmine - 10 - 10 - 9;
Pippa - 7 - 6 - 5;
Sean - 9 - 8 - 7.

No 18

The murder weapon in the fifth case wasn't a rock (clue 1), automobile (clue 2), poison (3) or a gun (5), so a knife. The weapon in the first case wasn't a rock (1) automobile (2) or poison (4), so a gun. Thus Dan Elder was murdered second (5). The weapon in the third case was a rock (1). Chloë Dean was murdered in her automobile (2), so hers was the fourth case, and Dan Elder was murdered with poison. Bob Cole was murdered first (4). Alf Barnet wasn't murdered fifth (3), so third. Emma Fry was murdered fifth.

Thus:

Alf Barnet - third - rock;
Bob Cole - first - gun;
Chloë Dean - fourth - automobile;
Dan Elder - second - poison;
Emma Fry - fifth - knife.

No 19

The Bule tribe lives in either territory B or territory D (clue 1) as does the Tupin tribe (clue 2) who found the canoe paddle. Thus the Bule tribe didn't find the airbed (4). The Conji tribe found a shoe (3), so the tribe which found the airbed is the Fora (4) who don't live in territory A (2), so they're in C (4) and the Yalom live in E. Thus the Conji are in A. The Bule found the beachball (1) and the Yalom found the oildrum. Territory B doesn't belong to the Bule tribe (5), so the Tupin tribe lives in B and the Bule tribe is in territory D.

Thus:

Territory A - Conji - shoe;
Territory B - Tupin - canoe paddle;
Territory C - Fora - airbed;
Territory D - Bule - beachball;
Territory E - Yalom - oildrum.

Solutions

No 20

Remember throughout that no-one married in November (grid). Thus either Ritchie married in October and the Rooks married in August (clue 1) or Ritchie married in December and the Rooks married in October. In other words, the October wedding was either Ritchie's or that of Mr and Mrs Rook. Leanne is neither Ritchie's wife nor Mrs Rook (clue 1), so Leanne married in September (2) and Carol married in August. Rosa thus married in October (3) and Daniel married in September. By elimination, Suzi married in December. Rosa's surname is Ward (3), so (1 and above) the Rooks married in August and Ritchie married in October. Mr Rook isn't Thomas (1), so Martin. Suzi is married to Thomas. Thomas is Mr Green (2), so Daniel is Mr Baker.

Thus:

Daniel - Baker - Leanne - September;
Martin - Rook - Carol - August;
Ritchie - Ward - Rosa - October;
Thomas - Green - Suzi - December.

No 21

Pamela's party found guns (clue 2) and Robert's found pottery (clue 3). Benjamin's didn't find silver (1), so rum. Fiona's party thus found silver. The *Barbera* sank in 1902 (4). The ship which sank in 1922 wasn't the *Lucy Jane* (1) or the *Warwick* (3), so the *Fontaine*. Benjamin's party didn't explore the *Fontaine* (1), so he explored the ship which sank in 1902 (*Barbera*, 4) and Fiona (silver, above) explored the ship which sank in 1862. The ship explored by Robert didn't sink in 1922 (3), so 1882. Thus Pamela explored the *Fontaine* (1922, above). The *Warwick* wasn't explored by Robert's party (3), so Fiona's explored the *Warwick* and Robert's party explored the *Lucy Jane*.

Thus:

Benjamin - *Barbera* - 1902 - rum;
Fiona - *Warwick* - 1862 - silver;
Pamela - *Fontaine* - 1922 - guns;
Robert - *Lucy Jane* - 1882 - pottery.

No 22

The person organizing a party on the 8th isn't Helen or Greta (clue 1), Isabel (since no party is on the 14th, grid and clue 2) or Tim (3), so Donald. Helen's party celebrates her new house (1). The birthday party isn't Donald's, Isabel's or Greta's (2), so Tim's. It isn't on the 29th (3), so the 19th (2) and Isabel's is on the 13th. Helen's is on the 23rd (1) and Greta's is on the 29th. Isabel's isn't celebrating a graduation or retirement (2), so an anniversary. The graduation party is thus on the 8th (1), so the retirement party is on the 29th.

Thus:

8th - graduation - Donald;
13th - anniversary - Isabel;
19th - birthday - Tim;
23rd - new house - Helen;
29th - retirement - Greta.

No 23

Bold Bill robbed near Northwood (clue 1). Storm was ridden by Artful Al (clue 4). Lightning's rider who robbed near Sandbridge wasn't Daring Dan (3) or Fearless Frank (2), so Evil Edmund. The owner of Brown Bess wasn't Bold Bill (1) or Fearless Frank (2), so Daring Dan.

Solutions

He didn't rob near Appleford (1) or Bunbury (3), so Oakton. Fearless Frank didn't ride Moonbeam (5), so Fleetfoot. He didn't rob near Appleford (5), so Bunbury. Bold Bill thus rode Moonbeam and Artful Al robbed near Appleford.

Thus:

Artful Al - Storm - Appleford;
Bold Bill - Moonbeam - Northwood;
Daring Dan - Brown Bess - Oakton;
Evil Edmund - Lightning - Sandbridge;
Fearless Frank - Fleetfoot - Bunbury.

No 24

Eric has either the jack or queen of hearts and Ken has either the 5 or 8 of diamonds (clue 1), so the man with the 6 of clubs and queen of diamonds (clue 2) plus either the ace or 5 of hearts is Patrick. Roy has either the 4 or 8 of clubs (2), so Ken has the jack of hearts (3) and jack of clubs. Eric has the queen of hearts. Ken has the 5 of diamonds (3) and Eric has the 8 of clubs. Roy has the 4 of clubs. Thus Patrick has the ace of hearts (2) and Roy has the 5 of hearts. The man with the king of diamonds isn't Roy (4), so Eric. Roy has the 8 of diamonds.

Thus (heart - club - diamond):

Eric - queen - 8 - king;
Ken - jack - jack - 5;
Patrick - ace - 6 - queen;
Roy - 5 - 4 - 8.

No 25

Joe Painter's client is Mrs Farmer (clue 1). The tiler isn't Sam Tiler (intro), so Sam Tiler's client isn't Mr Smith (clue 1). Sam Tiler's client isn't Miss Baker (4), so Mr Butcher who (1) lives in Wood Way. Andy

Joiner is working in Copper Lane (2). The joiner working in Slate Street isn't Mark Plumber (3), so Joe Painter. Thus Mark Plumber is working in Brick Road. His client isn't Miss Baker (4), so Mr Smith, thus Mark Plumber is the tiler (1). Andy Joiner's client is Miss Baker. Andy Joiner isn't the painter (2), so the plumber. Sam Tiler is the painter.

Thus:

Andy Joiner - plumber - Miss Baker - Copper Lane;
Joe Painter - joiner - Mrs Farmer - Slate Street;
Mark Plumber - tiler - Mr Smith - Brick Road;
Sam Tiler - painter - Mr Butcher - Wood Way.

No 26

Sue Sheldon is opening a store on Thursday (clue 3). The person booked for Monday's opening isn't Dale Drew (clue 1), Will Walters or Fionna Finn (2), so Polly Piper. Dale Drew is thus booked for Wednesday (1) and Polly Piper is the movie director. Will Walters will open a store on Friday (2) and Fionna Finn is booked for Tuesday. Will Walters is an actor (2), so Sue Sheldon is an author (1). Dale Drew isn't a singer (4), so a hockey player. Fionna Finn is the singer.

Thus:

Dale Drew - hockey player - Wednesday;
Fionna Finn - singer - Tuesday;
Polly Piper - movie director - Monday;
Sue Sheldon - author - Thursday;
Will Walters - actor - Friday.

Solutions

No 27

Tammy's surname is Earl (clue 2). Her husband isn't Adam (clue 1), Keith (2), Barry (3) or Wayne (4), so Rob. Adam's surname is King (1) and Barry's is Duke (3). Sue and her husband Wayne aren't surnamed Prince (4), so Lord. Keith's surname is Prince. Maggie isn't married to Adam (1). Maggie is older than Beryl (1), so Maggie isn't married to Barry (3). Thus Maggie's husband is Keith. Beryl's husband isn't Barry (3), so Adam. Lorraine is married to Barry.

Thus:

Beryl - Adam - King;
Lorraine - Barry - Duke;
Maggie - Keith - Prince;
Sue - Wayne - Lord;
Tammy - Rob - Earl.

No 28

Lisa has blonde hair (clue 1). The child with brown hair isn't Jane or Damien (clue 3), so Nicholas. The child with ginger hair isn't Damien (2), so Jane. Damien's hair is black. Jane is 11 (2), so Nicholas is 10 (3). Lisa isn't two years younger than Nicholas (1), so Lisa is 12 and Damien is 8. Child 4 (furthest right) isn't Lisa (1), Damien (2) or Nicholas (3), so Jane. Thus Nicholas is child 1 and Damien is child 3 (3). Child 2 is Lisa.

Thus:

Child 1 - Nicholas - 10 - brown;
Child 2 - Lisa - 12 - blonde;
Child 3 - Damien - 8 - black;
Child 4 - Jane - 11 - ginger.

No 29

George didn't use 5 or 6 petals (clue 2) or 8 or 9 ferns. Thus George didn't use 7 petals (clue 4).

So George used 8 petals, plus (4) 5 leaves. The child who used 4 leaves isn't Boris (1) or Marie (3), so Diana. George didn't use 7 ferns (2), so 6. Thus Boris used 7 ferns (1) and 7 leaves. Marie used 6 leaves, so (3) Diana used 6 petals. Boris used 5 petals (1), so Marie used 7 petals. Thus Marie used 8 ferns (4), so Diana used 9 ferns.

Thus (ferns - leaves - petals):

Boris - 7 - 7 - 5;
Diana - 9 - 4 - 6;
George - 6 - 5 - 8;
Marie - 8 - 6 - 7.

No 30

Remember throughout that each new picture is made of pieces of three old ones (intro). Louise's legs and Philip's body are in the same picture (clue 4). They're not with Hannah's head (clue 3) or David's head (4), so Christina's. Hannah's head is with Christina's legs (3), but not with David's body, so Louise's body. Hannah's body isn't with David's legs (2), so Philip's legs. By elimination, David's body is with Hannah's legs; and Christina's body is with David's legs. Christina's body isn't with Louise's head (1), so Philip's. David's head is thus with Hannah's body, and Louise's head is with David's body.

Thus (head - body - legs):

Christina - Philip - Louise;
David - Hannah - Philip;
Hannah - Louise - Christina;
Louise - David - Hannah;
Philip - Christina - David.

No 31

Boat B hasn't been hired for 15 days (clue 2), so boat B has been hired for 10 days (clue 3) and boat

Solutions

A for 5 days. The Hoopers aren't in boat A (1), so the Dunns have hired for 5 days and the Hoopers for 7 days. The family which has hired for 15 days is in boat D (2) and the Fishers are in B. The Wallace family have hired a boat for 3 days (4) and the Taylor family for 15 days. The Hoopers are in boat E (1) and the Wallaces are in C.
Thus:
Boat A - Dunn - 5 days;
Boat B - Fisher - 10 days;
Boat C - Wallace - 3 days;
Boat D - Taylor - 15 days;
Boat E - Hooper - 7 days.

No 32

Roberta's date isn't at 7.15pm (clue 1), so Ronnie's isn't at 7.00pm. The boy meeting a girl at 7.00pm isn't Darren (clue 2) or Neil (4), so Laurence. Thus the couple going to the cinema are meeting at 7.30pm (3) and Amber is meeting her date at 7.15pm. Darren is thus meeting his date at 7.30pm (2), the couple going to the dance are meeting at 7.15pm, and Nadine is meeting her date at 7.00pm. Roberta is meeting her date at 7.30pm (1), Ronnie is meeting his at 7.15pm, and the couple going to a restaurant are meeting at 7.00pm. By elimination, Neil is meeting Juliet at 7.45pm and taking her bowling.
Thus:
Darren - Roberta - 7.30pm - cinema;
Laurence - Nadine - 7.00pm - restaurant;
Neil - Juliet - 7.45pm - bowling;
Ronnie - Amber - 7.15pm - dance.

No 33

Lucy didn't work on Tuesday (grid), so Monday's cake wasn't chocolate (clue 3). Nor was it coconut (clue 1) or raisin cake (2), so ginger. Friday's cake wasn't raisin (2) or chocolate (3), so coconut. Friday's fruit was a pear (1), so the orange was eaten on Thursday (3) and chocolate cake on Wednesday. Raisin cake was eaten on Thursday. The beef sandwich wasn't eaten on Friday or Wednesday (1) or Thursday (4), so Monday. Thus the cheese sandwich and banana (2) were eaten on Wednesday. The apple was eaten on Monday. Thursday's sandwich wasn't ham (3), so salad. The ham sandwich was eaten on Friday.
Thus:
Monday - ginger - apple - beef;
Wednesday - chocolate - banana - cheese;
Thursday - raisin - orange - salad;
Friday - coconut - pear - ham.

No 34

The boy aged 10 has a sister aged 7 (clue 3) and Janet Weller is 4 (clue 4), so John Brown is 11 (1) and Janet Brown is 12. Thus John Gorman is 6 (5) and the 8-year-old girl has a 5-year-old brother. Janet Courtney's brother is 5 (2) and she's 8. The boy aged 10 (sister aged 7, 3) is thus John Atkinson. Janet Gorman is 9. John Weller is 3.
Thus (Janet - John):
Atkinson - 7 - 10;
Brown - 12 - 11;
Courtney - 8 - 5;
Gorman - 9 - 6;
Weller - 4 - 3.

Solutions

No 35

The woman who finished first wasn't in lane 3 (clue 2) or 2 (clue 4), so lane 1 (3) and Sharon was in lane 3. The woman who finished fifth thus wasn't in lane 4 (1). Nor was she in lanes 3 (2) or 2 (4), so the woman in lane 5 was fifth. Sharon (lane 3, above) was fourth (2) and Debbie was third. Caroline was fifth (3). Lee was in lane 4 (1), so Debbie was in lane 2 and Toni was in lane 1 (first, above). Lee was second.

Thus:

Lane 1 - Toni - first;
Lane 2 - Debbie - third;
Lane 3 - Sharon - fourth;
Lane 4 - Lee - second;
Lane 5 - Caroline - fifth.

No 36

Dick's surname is Duke (clue 1) and Dean's is Doran (clue 2). Doug's isn't Dance (3), so Derby. Dave is Mr Dance, who (3) forgot his lines. The man dismissed for throwing tantrums isn't Dick or Dean (1), so Doug. The one dismissed for drunkenness isn't Dean (2), so Dick. Dean was dismissed for absenteeism. The man dismissed in 2010 isn't Dick (2), who was dismissed later than Doug (1), who left the year before Dave (3). So Dick left in 2009, Dave in 2008 (3) and Doug in 2007. Dean was dismissed in 2010.

Thus:

Dave - Dance - 2008 - forgot lines;
Dean - Doran - 2010 - absenteeism;
Dick - Duke - 2009 - drunkenness;
Doug - Derby - 2007 - tantrums.

No 37

The person who received 21 (fewest) cards isn't Noelle or Stephen (clue 2), so Emmanuel (clue 4), and Gloria received 23. Gloria didn't send 25 (5), so (clues 2 and 3) Stephen sent 25, Emmanuel sent 26 and Noelle sent 27. Gloria sent 28. Emmanuel bought five fewer than Stephen (2), but ten more than Gloria (4), so Emmanuel bought 40, Stephen bought 45 and Gloria bought 30. Noelle bought 35. Stephen didn't get 22 (1), so 24. Noelle got 22.

Thus (bought - sent - received):

Emmanuel - 40 - 26 - 21;
Gloria - 30 - 28 - 23;
Noelle - 35 - 27 - 22;
Stephen - 45 - 25 - 24.

No 38

Monday's song wasn't *Losing You* (clue 1), *Only You* (clue 2), *No, No, No* or *Keep Cool* (3), so *My Dream*. Tuesday's wasn't *Losing You* (1), *Only You* (2) or *Keep Cool* (3), so *No, No, No*. Dave Dyme was in the studio on Monday (3). Friday's singer wasn't Fiona Fay or Gina Gould (1) or Ed Engles (2), so Harry Hibbert. *Keep Cool* was recorded on Thursday (4). Wednesday's song wasn't *Losing You* (1), so *Only You*. *Losing You* was recorded on Friday. Gina Gould sang on Thursday (1). Ed Engles didn't sing *Only You* (2), so his recording was on Tuesday. Fiona Fay sang on Wednesday.

Thus:

Monday - Dave Dyme - *My Dream*;
Tuesday - Ed Engles - *No, No, No*;
Wednesday - Fiona Fay - *Only You*;
Thursday - Gina Gould - *Keep Cool*;
Friday - Harry Hibbert - *Losing You*.

Solutions

No 39

The fifth train was pulled by *Kinlet Hall* (clue 2) and the fifth photo wasn't of Llangollen or Arley. Nor was the fifth photo of the Severn Valley (clue 1), so (4) the fifth was of Ramsbottom and the fourth was of Levisham. The train at Levisham was pulled by *Sir Nigel Gresley* (1). The first picture wasn't of Llangollen (2) or Arley (3), so the Severn Valley. *Foxcote Manor* pulled the train taken second (1). *Erlestoke Manor* pulled the train taken first (3), so *King Edward I* pulled the third train. The third picture wasn't of Llangollen (5), so Arley. The picture of Llangollen was taken second.

Thus:
First - *Erlestoke Manor* - Severn Valley;
Second - *Foxcote Manor* - Llangollen;
Third - *King Edward I* - Arley;
Fourth - *Sir Nigel Gresley* - Levisham;
Fifth - *Kinlet Hall* - Ramsbottom.

No 40

No girl is 9 years old (grid). Thus Michelle is either 10 or 12 (clue 1) and the girl with a red toothbrush is 11. So the girl with a yellow toothbrush is 10 (clue 2) and Trudi who uses Ice Mint toothpaste is 11. Claire's toothbrush is white (3). She isn't 8 (3), so 12. Thus Frances is 8 and Michelle is 10. By elimination, Frances has a blue toothbrush. Frances uses Fresh Mint (1). Claire doesn't use Mild Mint (3), so Cool Mint. Michelle uses Mild Mint toothpaste.

Thus:
Claire - 12 - Cool Mint - white;
Frances - 8 - Fresh Mint - blue;
Michelle - 10 - Mild Mint - yellow;
Trudi - 11 - Ice Mint - red.

No 41

Remember throughout that each woman's name and surname start with two different letters (intro) and that each woman is wearing two different colours. Beth's surname isn't Black or Brown (intro) or White (clue 1), so Green. Barbara's surname isn't Black or Brown (intro), so White. Mrs Black's skirt is brown and Beth's blouse is black (clue 4), thus Beth's skirt is green or white, as is Barbara's blouse (1). The woman in a brown blouse and black skirt (2) isn't Gina, so Wendy. Gina is Mrs Black (4) and Wendy is Ms Brown. Barbara's surname is White (above), so Gina's blouse is green (3). Thus Barbara's blouse is white, Beth's skirt is white (1) and Barbara's skirt is green.

Thus (blouse - skirt):
Barbara - White - white - green;
Beth - Green - black - white;
Gina - Black - green - brown;
Wendy - Brown - brown - black.

No 42

The clerk's car is either car 2 or car 3 (clue 1), as is the janitor's (clue 3). So car 1 is the manager's (3), car 2 is the janitor's and car 4 is Elizabeth's. Thus car 3 is the clerk's (1) and car 5 is the receptionist's. The accountant owns car 4. Car 2 is Dinah's (2). Richard's is car 1 (4) and Mike's is car 5. Car 3 belongs to Terence.

Solutions

Thus:
Car 1 - Richard - manager;
Car 2 - Dinah - janitor;
Car 3 - Terence - clerk;
Car 4 - Elizabeth - accountant;
Car 5 - Mike - receptionist.

No 43

Remember throughout that no bottle produces the note it should (intro) as indicated in the diagram. Thus the brown bottle produces the note G (clue 1). Bottle 7 produces E (clue 3). The one which produces F isn't 9 (intro), so bottle 5 produces F (2), bottle 3 is purple and bottle 1 is yellow and produces D. Bottle 3 doesn't produce G (intro), so B. Bottle 9 produces G. Bottle 7 isn't green (3), so blue. Bottle 5 is green.
Thus:
Bottle 1 - D - yellow;
Bottle 3 - B - purple;
Bottle 5 - F - green;
Bottle 7 - E - blue;
Bottle 9 - G - brown.

No 44

Ruby's heart isn't the queen (clue 1), so the king (clue 4). Ruby hasn't the jack of clubs (1), so Jeanne's heart is the ace (2) and the woman with the 2 of hearts has the jack of clubs. The woman with the jack of clubs isn't Gemma (3), so Carol. Gemma has the queen of hearts and (1) either the 9 or 10 of spades, and Ruby has either the 6 or 7 of clubs. Gemma has either the 6 or 7 of clubs (3), so Jeanne has the king of clubs. Ruby has either the 9 or 10 of spades (3). Carol hasn't the jack of spades (5), so the queen. Jeanne has the jack of spades. Gemma hasn't the 7 of clubs (6), so Ruby has the 7 and

Gemma has the 6 of clubs. Gemma has the 10 of spades (1), so Ruby has the 9 of spades.
Thus (heart - club - spade):
Carol - 2 - jack - queen;
Gemma - queen - 6 - 10;
Jeanne - ace - king - jack;
Ruby - king - 7 - 9.

No 45

Remember throughout that each woman made three different quantities (intro). Paula made 16 'other' cards (clue 2), so not 16 Christmas cards or 16 birthday cards. The woman who made 16 birthday cards isn't Sheryl or Teresa (clue 1), so Rowena. The woman who made 19 'other' cards isn't Rowena (1) or Teresa (2), so Sheryl. Thus Rowena (16 birthday cards, above) made 18 'other' cards (1), so Teresa made 17 'other' cards (1). Paula didn't make 16 Christmas cards and Rowena didn't make 18 (intro), so Rowena made 19 (2) and Paula made 18 Christmas cards. Teresa didn't make 17 Christmas cards (intro), so 16. Sheryl made 17 Christmas cards. Sheryl didn't make 17 birthday cards (intro), so Sheryl made 18 birthday cards (1) and Teresa made 19. Paula made 17 birthday cards.
Thus (birthday - Christmas - other):
Paula - 17 - 18 - 16;
Rowena - 16 - 19 - 18;
Sheryl - 18 - 17 - 19;
Teresa - 19 - 16 - 17.

No 46

Adam gets the lunch on Wednesday (clue 4). The person who gets lunch on Monday isn't Stephanie or William (clue 1) or

Solutions

Jenny (2), so Maurice, whose day off (3) is Wednesday. Stephanie collects lunch on Tuesday (1). Since Maurice's day off is Wednesday (above), Jenny's day off is Tuesday (2) and William's day off is Monday. Adam's day off is Friday (4) and Stephanie's is on Thursday. William gets lunch on Thursday (1), so Jenny gets lunch on Friday.

Thus (lunch - day off):
Adam - Wednesday - Friday;
Jenny - Friday - Tuesday;
Maurice - Monday - Wednesday;
Stephanie - Tuesday - Thursday;
William - Thursday - Monday.

No 47

The person at No 1 isn't Charles or George (clue 1) or Shane (clue 3). So Emma lives at No 1 (3) and Janice at No 2. The person using yellow paint lives due north of Charles (1), so Charles isn't using blue paint (2). Nor is his paint green (2) or white (4), so red. The person at No 9 isn't using yellow or red (1), green or blue (2), so white paint. George lives at either No 8 or No 9 (1) and Charles at either No 7 or No 8. George's paint isn't yellow (1), green (2) or blue (4), so white (No 9, above). Charles thus lives at No 8 (1) and Janice (No 2, above) is using yellow paint. Shane lives at No 7, so his paint is blue (2) and Emma's is green.

Thus:
No 1 - Emma - green;
No 2 - Janice - yellow;
No 7 - Shane - blue;
No 8 - Charles - red;
No 9 - George - white.

No 48

The woman who bought 3 (fewest) flowers isn't Gemma (clue 2), Marcia (clue 3) or Chris (4), so Diane. Gemma bought 4 (2). Diane didn't buy irises (2), so the woman who chose irises bought 5 (1) and someone bought 7 carnations. Chris bought flowers on Wednesday (4). The woman who bought flowers on Tuesday isn't Diane or Marcia (3), so Gemma. Diane bought roses (3), so Gemma bought poppies. Monday's shopper wasn't Diane (2), so Marcia. Diane bought flowers on Thursday. Chris bought irises (2), so Marcia bought carnations.

Thus:
Chris - irises - 5 - Wednesday;
Diane - roses - 3 - Thursday;
Gemma - poppies - 4 - Tuesday;
Marcia - carnations - 7 - Monday.

No 49

Ray's cracker didn't contain a pencil (clue 4), so Barry is the MAN (clue 1) whose cracker contained a pencil. Ray's had a mirror and a blue hat (2), so Barry's had an angel on the front. Ray's had a robin (4) and Barry's contained the red hat. Sharon's hat wasn't yellow (3), so green. Louise's hat was yellow. Sharon's cracker didn't have holly on the front (1), so Santa. Louise's had holly. Louise's contained a keyring (3), so Sharon's contained a whistle.

Thus:
Barry - angel - red - pencil;
Louise - holly - yellow - keyring;
Ray - robin - blue - mirror;
Sharon - Santa - green - whistle.

Solutions

No 50

Remember throughout that each new picture is made of pieces of three old ones (intro). Maggie's brother's head is with her aunt's body (clue 3), so not her aunt's or brother's legs. Her aunt's legs aren't with grandpa's head (clue 1) or mother's head (2), so her father's head. Her mother's head is with her father's body (2). Her grandpa's legs are with her mother's body (4), and (by elimination) her aunt's head. Her grandpa's head is thus with her brother's body. So her father's head is with her grandpa's body, her grandpa's head is with her brother's body, and her mother's head is with her brother's legs. Her father's legs are with her grandpa's head (1), so her mother's legs are with her brother's head.

Thus (head - body - legs):
Aunt - mother - grandpa;
Brother - aunt - mother;
Father - grandpa - aunt;
Grandpa - brother - father;
Mother - father - brother.

No 51

No-one has a hobby which begins with the same letter as that of his or her name (intro). Rhona's hobby is painting (clue 3). The person who enjoys cooking thus isn't Paul (clue 1). Nor is he/she Carol (intro) or Walter (1), so Gordon's hobby is cooking. Walter's is gardening (1), thus Walter and Paul are both on a different side of the table to Carol (1 and 2), so Carol's hobby isn't walking (2). Thus Carol's is reading and Paul's is walking. Paul is in seat E (3), so Walter is in D (1) and Carol is in B (2). Rhona isn't in A (3), so C. Gordon is in seat A.

Thus:
Seat A - Gordon - cooking;
Seat B - Carol - reading;
Seat C - Rhona - painting;
Seat D - Walter - gardening;
Seat E - Paul - walking.

No 52

Remember throughout that each family is made up of four people whose names begin with four different letters (intro). Freddie's sister isn't Fern or Camilla (clue 1) and Clive's wife isn't Cathy or Fran. Camilla's brother isn't Irwin (clue 2), so (by elimination) he's Paul. Irwin's mother is Polly (2), so (by elimination) his sister is Fern, thus their father is Clive. Freddie's sister is Patricia (1), so their father is Ian and their mother is Cathy. By elimination, Frank's wife is Ingrid and Peter's wife is Fran. Peter's son is Colin and Frank's son is Paul. Frank's daughter is Camilla and Peter's daughter is Isla.

Thus (husband - wife - son - daughter):
Clive - Polly - Irwin - Fern;
Frank - Ingrid - Paul - Camilla;
Ian - Cathy - Freddie - Patricia;
Peter - Fran - Colin - Isla.

No 53

Jade came second in geography (clue 2), so not first in geography. Her surname isn't Cole (clue 2), so Erica wasn't first in geography (1). The girl who was first in geography isn't Lucy (6), so Sue. The girl who came first in English was second in mathematics (5). Sue wasn't second in English (4), so history. Miss Sampson was first in history (3) and second in geography, so she's Jade. Lucy wasn't second in

Solutions

mathematics (6), so English; thus she was first in mathematics. Erica was first in English and second in mathematics. Lucy's surname is Cole (1). Sue's isn't Morris (4), so Brown. Erica's surname is Morris.

Thus (first - second):

Erica - Morris - English - mathematics;

Jade - Sampson - history - geography;

Lucy - Cole - mathematics - English;

Sue - Brown - geography - history.

No 54

No flight is delayed for 3 hours (grid). The person with a one-hour delay isn't Roger (clue 2), Eve (clue 3), Keith or Alan (4), so Marilyn. The flight to Turkey is delayed by 4 hours (1), so the 5-hour delay isn't Eve's (3). The person delayed for 5 hours isn't Keith or Alan (4), so Roger. The flight to Australia is delayed for 6 hours (2). The person going to Portugal isn't Roger or Marilyn (2), so (by elimination) the flight to Portugal is delayed by 2 hours. By elimination, Marilyn and/or Roger are going to Finland and/or Japan. Keith isn't going to Portugal (4), so his flight is delayed by 4 hours and Alan's is delayed by 6 hours. Eve is thus going to Portugal, so (3) Marilyn is going to Finland. Roger is travelling to Japan.

Thus:

Alan - Australia - 6 hours;

Eve - Portugal - 2 hours;

Keith - Turkey - 4 hours;

Marilyn - Finland - 1 hour;

Roger - Japan - 5 hours.

No 55

Apricot bath oil wasn't used with rose (clue 1), wisteria or lilac (clue 4) or violet talc (5), so lavender talc. They weren't used on Monday or Tuesday (2), so Wednesday (5), almond oil was used on Thursday and violet talc on Friday. Magnolia oil was used on Tuesday (2). Strawberry oil wasn't used with rose (3), wisteria or lilac (4), so violet talc. Thus lily oil was used on Monday. Rose talc wasn't used on Monday or Tuesday (3), so Thursday. Wisteria talc wasn't used on Monday (3), so Tuesday. Lilac talc was used on Monday.

Thus (bath oil - talc):

Monday - lily - lilac;

Tuesday - magnolia - wisteria;

Wednesday - apricot - lavender;

Thursday - almond - rose;

Friday - strawberry - violet.

No 56

The woman who has been working for 2 hours isn't Naomi (clue 1), Shelley (clue 2) or Grace (3), so Holly. Her picture isn't of a cat (1), dogs (2) or flowers (4), so horses, and Miss Grove has been working for 3 hours on a picture of flowers. Shelley's picture is of dogs (2). Miss Roper has been working for 2 hours (3) and Grace for 5 hours, so Naomi is Mrs Grove. By elimination, Grace's picture is of a cat and Shelley has been working for 6 hours. Shelley's surname isn't White (2), so Maloney. Grace is Mrs White.

Thus:

Grace - White - cat - 5 hours;

Holly - Roper - horses - 2 hours;

Naomi - Grove - flowers - 3 hours;

Shelley - Maloney - dogs - 6 hours.

Solutions

No 57

Remember throughout that each couple is moving from and to two different towns (intro). Hal is married to Katy (clue 4). Laura's husband isn't Ian (clue 1) or Jack (2), so Geoff. Geoff isn't moving from or to Broadfield or Dinsdale (3), so the man going from Broadfield isn't Ian (1) and the one going to Dinsdale isn't Jack (2). So Hal and Katy are moving from Broadfield to Dinsdale. Naomi is moving to Broadfield (4), thus her husband isn't Jack (2), so Ian. Jack's wife is Molly. The man moving from Dinsdale isn't Ian (1), so Jack. He isn't moving to Applewood (5), so Cliff Point. Geoff is moving to Applewood, so (1) Ian is moving from Applewood, and Geoff is moving from Cliff Point.

Thus (from - to):

Geoff - Laura - Cliff Point - Applewood;

Hal - Katy - Broadfield - Dinsdale;

Ian - Naomi - Applewood - Broadfield;

Jack - Molly - Dinsdale - Cliff Point.

No 58

Abigail received slippers (clue 1). Brenda gave perfume (clue 2) and didn't receive a clock. Nor did she receive a book (3), so Brenda received a watch. Abigail didn't give a watch (3), nor was the watch given by Georgina (4) or Fern (5), so Harriet gave the watch and (3) received a book from Georgina (4). Abigail didn't give slippers (she received them, 1), so Abigail gave a clock. Fern gave slippers. Brenda didn't give to Georgina (4), so Fern. Abigail gave a present to Georgina.

Thus (donor - recipient):

Abigail - Georgina - clock;

Brenda - Fern - perfume;

Fern - Abigail - slippers;

Georgina - Harriet - book;

Harriet - Brenda - watch.

No 59

Basket A contains 12 oranges and 6 lemons (clue 4), so basket D contains 14 oranges and 8 lemons (clue 3). Basket C contains 10 lemons (2) and basket E contains 14, so basket B contains 12 lemons. The total number of oranges plus lemons in A is 18, and the total number in D is 22, so the total in B (12 lemons, above) isn't 18 or 22 (1), thus basket B contains 8 oranges, so a total of 20 oranges plus lemons. Thus basket C (10 lemons, above) hasn't 10 oranges (1), so 6 oranges. Basket E thus contains 10 oranges.

Thus (oranges - lemons):

Basket A - 12 - 6;

Basket B - 8 - 12;

Basket C - 6 - 10;

Basket D - 14 - 8;

Basket E - 10 - 14.

No 60

No child complained after 10 kilometres (grid), so the 7-year-old complained after either 4 or 6 kilometres (clue 2). Roy complained after either 8 or 12 kilometres (clue 3), so he isn't 7. Thus Roy is 8 (3) and Laura is 6. The child who complained after 4 kilometres isn't 5 (1), nor is he/she Laura (2), so the child who complained after 4 kilometres is 7 years old. Laura who was bored (2) complained after 6 kilometres. The child who was too cold thus complained after

Solutions

4 kilometres (1) and the 5-year-old complained after 8 kilometres. Roy thus complained after 12 kilometres. Adam is 5 (3), so Gillian is 7. Adam wasn't too hot (3), so he was car sick. Roy was too hot.
Thus:
Adam - 5 - car sick - 8 kilometres;
Gillian - 7 - too cold - 4 kilometres;
Laura - 6 - bored - 6 kilometres;
Roy - 8 - too hot - 12 kilometres.

No 61

The woman at No 5 isn't Fran (clue 2), Denise (clue 3) or Abigail (4), so Glenda. Thus Denise lives at No 3 (3). Abigail doesn't live at No 2 (4), so No 4. By elimination, Fran lives at No 2. Denise isn't 34 (4), so Glenda (at No 5, above) is 34. Fran is 35 (3). The 33-year-old (youngest) isn't Abigail (2), so Denise. Abigail is thus 36. Denise (at No 3, above) hasn't 3 children (1) or 4 children (4), so 2 children (2) and Abigail has 3. Glenda (at No 5, above) hasn't 5 children (1), so 4. Fran has 5 children.
Thus:
No 2 - Fran - 35 - 5 children;
No 3 - Denise - 33 - 2 children;
No 4 - Abigail - 36 - 3 children;
No 5 - Glenda - 34 - 4 children.

No 62

The child in position A isn't Jimmy (clue 3), so Jason is in position A (clue 1) and the pattern on Jimmy's pyjamas is zigzags. Jason's pyjama pattern isn't stripes (1), circles (2) or flowers (3), so teddy bears. The child in seat B (next to Jason in A, above) isn't Jodie or Jimmy (3) or Jade (4), so Jemima. The girl with circles on her pyjamas is thus in position E (2). She isn't Jodie

(either left of Jimmy or wearing flower-patterned pyjamas, 3), so Jade. The child in position D thus isn't Jodie (4), so Jimmy. Jodie is in C. Jodie's pyjamas have stripes (1), so Jemima's have flowers.
Thus:
Position A - Jason - teddy bears;
Position B - Jemima - flowers;
Position C - Jodie - stripes;
Position D - Jimmy - zigzags;
Position E - Jade - circles.

No 63

The car which has been in the showroom for 5 months isn't the Mohotsu (clue 2), Diwitson (clue 3), Alvaro or Scarba (4), so the Prioto. It isn't priced at $110 (2), so the Alvaro has been in the showroom for 8 months (4), the $110 car for 6 months and the Scarba for 9 months. The $110 car isn't the Diwitson (3), so the Mohotsu. The Diwitson has thus been in the showroom for 7 months. The $150 car has thus been in the showroom for 5 months (3). The $140 car isn't the Alvaro (1), so the Diwitson (3) and the Scarba is priced at $130. The Alvaro is priced at $120.
Thus:
Alvaro - 8 months - $120;
Diwitson - 7 months - $140;
Mohotsu - 6 months - $110;
Prioto - 5 months - $150;
Scarba - 9 months - $130.

No 64

Mandy sent one fewer email to friends than Zara (clue 2), so (by elimination) Rose is the woman who sent 5 emails to family and one more to friends than Gayle (clue 1). The woman who sent 2 family emails isn't Zara (3) or Mandy (2),

Solutions

so Gayle. Zara sent 6 to her family
(2) and Mandy sent 9. Gayle sent 6
emails to friends (3), so Rose sent
7 (1), Mandy sent 3 (2) and Zara
sent 4 to friends. The woman who
sent 4 business emails isn't Gayle
or Mandy (2) or Zara (4), so Rose.
Thus Zara didn't send 6 business
emails (4). So Mandy sent 6 (2) and
Gayle sent 7. Zara sent 8 business
emails.

Thus (business - family - friends):
Gayle - 7 - 2 - 6;
Mandy - 6 - 9 - 3;
Rose - 4 - 5 - 7;
Zara - 8 - 6 - 4.

No 65

Remember throughout that every
combination has three different
digits (clue 1). The person whose
first digit is 2 isn't Fred (clue 2),
Mitch (3) or Cathy (4), so Pamela.
The person whose first is 3 isn't
Fred (2) or Cathy (4), so Mitch.
Mitch's third isn't 3 (1), so 2 (4) and
Cathy's third is 3. Fred's third isn't 5
(2), so 4. Pamela's third is 5. Fred's
first isn't 4 (1), so 5. Cathy's first is
4. Cathy's second digit isn't 3 or 4
(1) or 2 (5), so 5. Mitch's second
isn't 2 or 3 (1), so 4. Pamela's
second isn't 2 (1), so 3. Fred's
second digit is 2.

Thus (first - second - third):
Cathy - 4 - 5 - 3;
Fred - 5 - 2 - 4;
Mitch - 3 - 4 - 2;
Pamela - 2 - 3 - 5.

No 66

No candle is 8 centimetres tall or
11 centimetres tall (grid). Candle
A (furthest left) isn't pink or green
(clue 1), red (clue 2) or orange (3),
so white. Candle B isn't pink (1),

red (2) or orange (3), so green.
Thus A is 7 centimetres tall (1). B
is thus 9 centimetres tall (2) and
the red candle is 10 centimetres
tall. The red candle is thus 3
centimetres taller than the white
candle, so the red candle isn't E
(3). The red candle isn't C (2), so
D. Candle E is orange (3), so C is
pink. C is 12 centimetres tall (2), so
E is 6 centimetres tall.

Thus:
Candle A - 7cm - white;
Candle B - 9cm - green;
Candle C - 12cm - pink;
Candle D - 10cm - red;
Candle E - 6cm - orange.

No 67

The person at No 5 isn't Rick or
Stella (clue 1), Marie (clue 2) or
Leo (3), so Pauline. Rick lives at
either No 1 or No 3 (1), as does
Leo (3), so Marie and/or Stella live
at either No 2 and/or No 4. Either
the driver of the red car is at No 1
and the driver of the green car lives
at No 3 (2) or the driver of the red
car lives at No 3 and the driver of
the green car lives at No 5; either
way, the person who lives at No 3
drives a green or red car. Thus Leo
doesn't live at No 1 (3). So Leo is
at No 3 (above), the person at No 5
(Pauline, above) has a blue car (3)
and the one at No 4 has a silver
car. Rick lives at No 1. Leo's car is
green (2), Rick's is red and Marie
lives at No 2. Stella lives at No 4.
Marie's car is black.

Thus:
No 1 - Rick - red;
No 2 - Marie - black;
No 3 - Leo - green;
No 4 - Stella - silver;
No 5 - Pauline - blue.

Solutions

No 68

Remember throughout that each new picture is made of pieces of four old ones (intro). Aunt Betty's feet are attached to either Uncle Kevin's legs or Uncle Stan's legs (clue 1). Uncle Stan's head and Uncle Kevin's body are in the same picture (clue 2), thus they're with the legs of a woman. So they're not with Aunt Betty's feet (above), thus they're with Aunt Helen's feet and Aunt Betty's legs. Uncle Kevin's head isn't with Aunt Helen's legs (3), so Uncle Stan's legs. By elimination, they're with Aunt Betty's feet and Aunt Helen's body. So Aunt Helen's head is with Aunt Betty's body, Uncle Kevin's legs and Uncle Stan's feet. Aunt Betty's head is with Uncle Stan's body, Aunt Helen's legs and Uncle Kevin's feet.

Thus (head - body - legs - feet):
Aunt Betty - Uncle Stan -
   Aunt Helen - Uncle Kevin;
Aunt Helen - Aunt Betty -
   Uncle Kevin - Uncle Stan;
Uncle Kevin - Aunt Helen -
   Uncle Stan - Aunt Betty;
Uncle Stan - Uncle Kevin -
   Aunt Betty - Aunt Helen.

No 69

Lou hasn't the 7 of spades (clue 3), so Lou has the 4 of spades (clue 1), Katy has the 10 of clubs and Sarah has the 8 of diamonds. Thus Katy has the 7 of spades (2), Anna has the jack of diamonds, and the woman with the ace of spades has the 9 of clubs. Anna hasn't the ace of spades (2), so Anna has the queen of spades. Sarah has the ace of spades. Katy has the 5 of diamonds (3) and Lou has the 7 of diamonds. Anna has the jack of

diamonds (above), so Lou has the 6 of clubs (4) and Anna has the king of clubs.

Thus (club - diamond - spade):
Anna - king - jack - queen;
Katy - 10 - 5 - 7;
Lou - 6 - 7 - 4;
Sarah - 9 - 8 - ace.

No 70

No appointment was at 10.15am (grid). The students with the appointments at 9.45am and 10.00am weren't Kevin (clue 2), George (clue 3) or Henry (4), so either Ivor or Jack. The 10.30am appointment wasn't Kevin's (2) or Henry's (4), so George's. Thus the student assessed as 'superb' was seen at 10.00am (3). The 'steady' student was seen at 9.45am (2) and Kevin at 10.45am. Henry was thus seen at 11.00am. Kevin's progress was assessed as 'slow' (2), so George's was 'shameful' (1) and Jack saw Professor Crammer at 9.45am. Thus Ivor saw him at 10.00am. Henry's progress was assessed as 'slapdash'.

Thus:
George - 10.30am - 'shameful';
Henry - 11.00am - 'slapdash';
Ivor - 10.00am - 'superb';
Jack - 9.45am - 'steady';
Kevin - 10.45am - 'slow'.

No 71

The girl with 15 bows has either 24 or 29 buttons (clue 3), so she isn't Fran (clue 2). Thus Fran has 26 bows (2) and the girl with 29 buttons has 15 bows. Amy has 18 buttons (3). Fran (26 bows, above) hasn't 7 buttons (1), so 13 (2) and

Solutions

Linda has 24 buttons. Tracey hasn't 7 buttons (1), so 29. Moira has 7 buttons. Moira hasn't 4 bows (3), so 9 (1). Amy has 4 (3), so Linda has 21 bows.

Thus (buttons - bows):

Amy - 18 - 4;

Fran - 13 - 26;

Linda - 24 - 21;

Moira - 7 - 9;

Tracey - 29 - 15.

No 72

Olivia was in either tent C or tent D (clue 4) and Laura was in either A or B. If Victoria was in A, then Nicole was in B (clue 2), leaving no room for Laura. So Laura was in A, Victoria in B, Nicole in C (2) and Olivia and (4) Tracey were in D. Adele and/or Colette were in either A and/or C (1), so Jessica was in B. The girls from Ottawa were in A (3). The girls from Toronto weren't in B or C (3), so D. The girls from Vancouver weren't in C (1), so B. Adele was thus in A (1), so Colette was in C. The girls in C were from Montreal.

Thus:

Tent A - Adele - Laura - Ottawa;

Tent B - Jessica - Victoria - Vancouver;

Tent C - Colette - Nicole - Montreal;

Tent D - Tracey - Olivia - Toronto.

No 73

No man had a birthday on Tuesday and no woman had a birthday on Wednesday (grid). The man whose birthday was on Friday isn't Ben (clue 1), Rodney or Jamie (clue 2), so Vince. The man whose wife's birthday was on Monday isn't Jamie or Rodney (2) or Ben (4), so Vince. The woman whose birthday was on Friday isn't Louise (3), Tina (4) or Sarah (5), so Cora. The woman whose birthday was on Thursday isn't Tina (4) or Sarah (5), so Louise. Thus Sarah's husband is Vince (3). By elimination, Tina's birthday was on Tuesday. Tina's husband isn't Ben (1) or Jamie (5), so Rodney. Jamie's birthday was on Monday (2). Ben's birthday was thus on Wednesday (1) and Rodney's was on Thursday. Jamie's wife's birthday was on Friday (2), so Jamie's wife is Cora. Ben's wife is Louise.

Thus (his - hers):

Ben - Louise - Wednesday - Thursday;

Jamie - Cora - Monday - Friday;

Rodney - Tina - Thursday - Tuesday;

Vince - Sarah - Friday - Monday.

No 74

The woman with the brown bag isn't Maureen, Vera or Thelma (clue 2) or Joan (clue 3), so Cindy. She isn't fourth or fifth (1) or first (2), so either second or third. The woman first in the queue isn't Maureen or Thelma (2) or Joan (3), so Vera. In clue 1, Vera is the woman with the black bag. In clue 2, the woman with the green bag isn't Maureen or Thelma, so Joan. Maureen's bag isn't blue (3), so red. Thelma's is blue. Joan isn't fourth or fifth (1), so she's second or third, as is Cindy (above). The woman directly in front of Joan hasn't a brown bag (3), so

Solutions

isn't Cindy. Thus Joan is second and Cindy is third. Maureen isn't fifth (3), so fourth. Thelma is fifth.
Thus:
First - Vera - black;
Second - Joan - green;
Third - Cindy - brown;
Fourth - Maureen - red;
Fifth - Thelma - blue.

No 75

Jill went to either Egypt in November or Portugal in December (clue 1), so either way, she didn't go to Venezuela in November (clue 2). Whoever went to Venezuela in November also went to either Brazil or Egypt in December (2) and isn't Lucy. Arthur went to either Venezuela in December or Egypt in November (3), so he didn't go to Venezuela in November (2). Kevin went to either Egypt or Greece in November (4). So Brian is the person who went to Venezuela in November and either Brazil or Egypt in December (2). Brian went to Brazil in December (3) and Arthur went to Egypt in November. Kevin went to Greece in November (4). Lucy went to Greece in December (2), so Arthur went to Venezuela in December (3). Jill went to Portugal in December (1), so Kevin went to Egypt in December. Since Jill went to Portugal in December (above), she didn't go to Portugal in November (intro), so to Brazil. Lucy went to Portugal in November.
Thus (November - December):
Arthur - Egypt - Venezuela;
Brian - Venezuela - Brazil;
Jill - Brazil - Portugal;
Kevin - Greece - Egypt;
Lucy - Portugal - Greece.

No 76

Toby was two places ahead of Zach (clue 4), so Marilyn was either two places ahead or two places behind Liz. The person between Liz and the pencil-buyer (clue 2) was thus either Toby or Zach, and the pencil-buyer was thus Marilyn. Toby wanted an eraser (4), so the person directly in front of Marilyn, who wanted a ruler (1) is Zach. Thus Liz wanted a notebook. Zach was one place ahead of Marilyn (1) and two places behind Toby (4), so Zach was third, Marilyn fourth and Toby first. Liz was second. Toby wanted 4 stamps (3), so Marilyn wanted 6 (1). Liz didn't want 5 (3), so 8. Zach wanted 5 stamps.
Thus:
Liz - second - 8 - notebook;
Marilyn - fourth - 6 - pencil;
Toby - first - 4 - eraser;
Zach - third - 5 - ruler.

No 77

No child has a birthday on Friday (grid) and no child is 6 years old. The child whose birthday is on Saturday isn't Ben (clue 1), Joanne (clue 3) or Alice (4), so Stephen, and (2) the child surnamed Grove has a birthday on Thursday. Stephen is either 8 or 9 (3), so Ben isn't two years older than Stephen (1), thus Ben's birthday is on Tuesday. Stephen's surname isn't Jackson (3) or Hibbert (4), so Ivy. Ben is thus the BOY (4) surnamed Hibbert. Joanne's surname isn't Jackson (3), so Grove. Alice's surname is Jackson, thus her birthday is on Wednesday (3). The 5-year-old isn't Ben (1) or Alice (3), so Joanne. Ben is 7 (1), so Stephen is 9 (3) and Alice is 8 years old.

Solutions

Thus:
Alice - Jackson - Wednesday - 8;
Ben - Hibbert - Tuesday - 7;
Joanne - Grove - Thursday - 5;
Stephen - Ivy - Saturday - 9.

No 78

The child who planted 22 snowdrops isn't Laura or Norman (clue 1), Katie (clue 3) or Joe (4), so Michael. The child who planted 20 snowdrops isn't Norman (1), Katie (3) or Joe (4), so Laura. Laura didn't plant 15 crocuses (4), so Katie planted 10 snowdrops (3) and the child who planted 15 crocuses also planted 14 snowdrops. Joe thus planted 14 snowdrops (4), so Laura planted 14 crocuses. Norman planted 16 snowdrops. Katie planted 10 crocuses (2), Norman planted 9 and Michael planted 13 crocuses.

Thus (crocuses - snowdrops):
Joe - 15 - 14;
Katie - 10 - 10;
Laura - 14 - 20;
Michael - 13 - 22;
Norman - 9 - 16.

No 79

Cheryl gave the egg in gold foil (clue 1). The one from Doug wasn't in blue (clue 1), silver or pink (2), so purple foil. Thus it was eaten directly before the egg from Benny (3). Thus Benny's wasn't in silver or pink foil (2), so blue. The eggs eaten fourth and fifth weren't wrapped in gold (1) or pink foil (2). Since Doug's was eaten directly before Benny's (above) the one in silver wasn't eaten fourth or fifth (2). So Doug's was eaten fourth and

Benny's was eaten fifth. The one in gold foil was eaten third (1), so the one in silver was eaten second (2) and the one in pink foil was eaten first. The egg in purple foil was eaten fourth (above), so the one from Stella wasn't eaten second (3). Thus Stella gave the egg in pink foil (eaten first, above) and that from Larry was wrapped in silver foil.

Thus:
Blue - Benny - fifth;
Gold - Cheryl - third;
Pink - Stella - first;
Purple - Doug - fourth;
Silver - Larry - second.

No 80

Person D isn't Donald (clue 1), Elizabeth (clue 2) or Vanessa (3), so Jason. Person A is neither Elizabeth (2) nor the one whose subject is politics (3), so Elizabeth is either B or C. Either way, the one whose subject is politics is thus D (3). So Elizabeth is B (3 and above). Donald is thus A (1) and Vanessa is C. B is the science expert (1) and Donald's surname is Wallis. Vanessa's is Porter (2) and Donald's subject is music, so Vanessa's is sport. Person B's surname isn't Scott (4), so Castle. Person D is surnamed Scott.

Thus:
Person A - Donald - Wallis - music;
Person B - Elizabeth - Castle - science;
Person C - Vanessa - Porter - sport;
Person D - Jason - Scott - politics.

No 81

Remember throughout that each child brought three different

Solutions

quantities (intro). Cheryl brought 6 flowers (clue 2) and the child who brought 7 berries brought 6 leaves. Darren brought 7 leaves (clue 3), the child who brought 9 flowers brought 6 leaves, and the child who brought 5 berries brought 8 leaves. By elimination, Darren brought 5 flowers, and the child who brought 4 leaves brought 6 berries, so the one who brought 7 leaves brought 4 berries. Thus Cheryl brought 8 leaves and the one who brought 7 flowers brought 6 berries. Andrew brought 4 leaves (1), so Emily brought 6 leaves.

Thus (berries - flowers - leaves):
Andrew - 6 - 7 - 4;
Cheryl - 5 - 6 - 8;
Darren - 4 - 5 - 7;
Emily - 7 - 9 - 6.

No 82

Either Samuel or Lola did the kitchen in August (clue 1), so Graeme did his bathroom in September (clue 3) and whichever of Samuel or Lola did the kitchen in August also did the bathroom in March. Lola did her bathroom in March (4) and Nigel did his kitchen in April. Nigel didn't do his bathroom in May (4). So Nigel did his bathroom in June (2) and Samuel did his kitchen in June. Deirdre did her bathroom in May (1), so Samuel did his in July. Deirdre didn't do her kitchen in July (2), so October. Graeme did his kitchen in July.

Thus (bathroom - kitchen):
Deirdre - May - October;
Graeme - September - July;
Lola - March - August;
Nigel - June - April;
Samuel - July - June.

No 83

The soap which is broadcast first on Wednesday isn't shown second on Wednesday (intro), the one broadcast first on Thursday isn't shown second on either Wednesday or Thursday, and the one broadcast first on Friday isn't shown second on either Wednesday, Thursday or Friday. The one shown first on Tuesday has its second episode on Sunday (clue 1), so (by elimination) the one shown first on Friday has its second episode on Saturday, the one shown first on Thursday is second on Friday, the one shown first on Wednesday is second on Thursday, and the one shown first on Monday is second on Wednesday. Both episodes of *Driftwood* are broadcast earlier in the week than both episodes of *Hospital Life* (clue 2).The first episode of *Hospital Life* is shown on either Thursday or Friday, as is the first episode of *Hobart Hill* (3). Thus the second episode of *The Saga* is shown on either Wednesday or Thursday (3), as is the second episode of *Driftwood*. So the first episode shown on Tuesday is of *Family Feud*. The second episode of *The Saga* is (by elimination) thus shown on Thursday (2), as is the first episode of *Hospital Life*. Thus *Driftwood* is shown on Monday and Wednesday (first and second) (2). The first episode of *Hobart Hill* is shown on Friday.

Thus (first - second):
Driftwood - Monday - Wednesday;
Family Feud - Tuesday - Sunday;
Hobart Hill - Friday - Saturday;
Hospital Life - Thursday - Friday;
The Saga - Wednesday - Thursday.

Solutions

No 84

Brick A isn't orange (clue 1) or pink (clue 2), so either brown or turquoise – thus brick B is neither brown nor turquoise (3). Brick B isn't pink (2), so orange. C has a picture of a leopard (1) and A has a number 7. A hasn't a picture of a fox (2) or an elephant (3), so an iguana. D hasn't a picture of a fox (2), so an elephant. The fox is on B. The 2 is on brick C (2). B has the number 3 (2) and 5 is on the pink brick, which is thus D. D has an elephant (above), so A is brown (3). Brick C is turquoise.

Thus:
Brick A - 7 - iguana - brown;
Brick B - 3 - fox - orange;
Brick C - 2 - leopard - turquoise;
Brick D - 5 - elephant - pink.

No 85

No girl babysits on Friday (grid). The girl who babysits on Saturday doesn't look after David (clue 1), Teresa (clue 2) or Louella (3), so Patrick. The child looked after on Tuesday isn't David (1) or Louella (3), so Teresa. Sheila babysits on Thursday (2), but not for the child aged 8 (oldest). Louella is 5 (3) and Jeanne babysits on Saturday (Patrick, above). The 8-year-old isn't David (1) or Patrick (3), so Teresa. David's babysitter isn't Barbara or Faith (1), so Sheila. Faith babysits on Wednesday (1), so Barbara babysits on Tuesday. Thus Faith looks after Louella. Jeanne babysits for the 7-year-old (2) and Sheila babysits for the 3-year-old. Patrick is 7 years old.

Thus:
Barbara - Teresa - 8 - Tuesday;
Faith - Louella - 5 - Wednesday;
Jeanne - Patrick - 7 - Saturday;
Sheila - David - 3 - Thursday.

No 86

Remember throughout that each new picture is made of pieces of three old ones (intro). Alleyn's legs are with Marple's body (clue 1) and Marple's legs are with Poirot's body (clue 3). Wimsey's legs aren't with Holmes's body (5), so Alleyn's. Thus Poirot's legs are with Holmes's body, and Holmes's legs are with Wimsey's body. Wimsey's head is with Poirot's legs (2). Marple's head isn't with Alleyn's body (1), so (by elimination) Marple's head is with Wimsey's body. Poirot's head isn't with Alleyn's legs (4), so Wimsey's legs. By elimination, Marple's body is with Holmes's head, and Poirot's body is with Alleyn's head.

Thus (head - body - legs):
Alleyn - Poirot - Marple;
Holmes - Marple - Alleyn;
Marple - Wimsey - Holmes;
Poirot - Alleyn - Wimsey;
Wimsey - Holmes - Poirot.

No 87

Colin has coffee (clue 5). The man with tea is sitting between Kenny (clue 2) and Harry (4), thus he isn't John (1). By elimination, Ivan has tea. The man with beer who is sitting clockwise of Ivan (3) is thus Harry (4), The man drinking water isn't John (1), so Kenny. John has

124

Solutions

cola. Thus John is in seat 1 (5), so Colin and Kenny (with water) are in either seats 2 and/or 5 (1). Since John has cola, Kenny isn't in seat 5 (2), so he's in seat 2 and Colin is in seat 5. Ivan is in seat 3 (2), so Harry is in seat 4.

Thus:

Seat 1 - John - cola;
Seat 2 - Kenny - water;
Seat 3 - Ivan - tea;
Seat 4 - Harry - beer;
Seat 5 - Colin - coffee.

No 88

Remember throughout that each woman bought three different quantities (intro). The woman who bought 4 bottles of red wine didn't buy 4 of white, so Leonie didn't buy 3 of white (clue 4). The woman who bought 3 white isn't Nadine (clue 1) or Olivia (3), so Madge. The woman who bought 5 white didn't buy 6 rosé (5), so the woman who bought 6 rosé thus bought either 3 or 4 white. Nadine bought either 4 or 5 white (1). The woman who bought 6 white isn't Leonie (4), so Olivia. Madge didn't buy 6 rosé (2), so 5 (5) and the woman who bought 5 white bought 3 rosé. Nadine didn't buy 6 rosé (1), so Leonie bought 6 rosé and (by elimination) 4 white, and Nadine bought 5 white (1). Olivia thus bought 4 rosé. Nadine bought 4 red (4), so Olivia bought 5 (3) and Madge bought 6 red. Leonie bought 3 bottles of red wine.

Thus (red - rosé - white):

Leonie - 3 - 6 - 4;
Madge - 6 - 5 - 3;
Nadine - 4 - 3 - 5;
Olivia - 5 - 4 - 6.

No 89

Thursday's group heard breaking glass (clue 4). The noise in the kitchen was on Tuesday (clue 5). The whistling in the ballroom wasn't heard on Wednesday (2), so Monday. If Thursday's group numbered 10 people, then those who heard a door banging numbered 7 (4), leaving no possible number for the party who toured on Monday (3). So there were 12 in Thursday's group (4) and 9 in the party that heard a door banging. Thus either the sound of breaking glass or that of a door banging was in the cellar (3). The footsteps weren't heard in the library (1), so the kitchen. Thus Wednesday's noise was the door banging. Monday's party was of 7 people (2). Wednesday's noise was in the cellar (3), so Thursday's was in the library. Tuesday's party was of 10 people.

Thus:

Monday - 7 - ballroom - whistling;
Tuesday - 10 - kitchen - footsteps;
Wednesday - 9 - cellar - door banging;
Thursday - 12 - library - breaking glass.

No 90

Remember throughout the quantities listed in the grid. The batch of 6 pots wasn't painted orange or green (clue 1) blue (clue 3) or brown (4), so yellow. Caroline made either 11 blue pots and 6 on Friday (3) or 16 blue pots and 11 on Friday; in other words, the batch of 11 pots was

Solutions

either blue or made on Friday. The brown pots weren't made on Friday (4), so there weren't 11 brown pots. Nor was the batch of 11 painted green or orange (1), so she made 11 blue pots and (3) 6 pots on Friday (yellow, above). There were either 16 green and 19 orange (1) or 19 green and 22 orange; in other words, the batch of 19 was either green or orange. There weren't 22 brown pots (4), so there were 16 brown pots, 19 green and 22 orange. The pots made on Thursday weren't green (2), orange (4) or brown (5), so blue and (2) the green pots were made on Tuesday. The brown pots were thus made on Wednesday (4) and the orange pots on Monday.

Thus:

Monday - 22 - orange;
Tuesday - 19 - green;
Wednesday - 16 - brown;
Thursday - 11 - blue;
Friday - 6 - yellow.

No 91

The fruit eaten on Monday wasn't the apple (clue 1), banana or pear (clue 2) or peach (3), so the pineapple. The fruit eaten on Tuesday wasn't the banana or pear (2) or peach (3), so the apple. The cashews were eaten on either Tuesday or Wednesday (3) and not with the banana or the peach. The pear was eaten on either Thursday or Friday (2), so not with the cashews (above). By elimination, the cashews were eaten with the apple, so (3) the brazils were eaten on Monday. The almonds weren't

eaten with the banana or pear (2), so the peach. They weren't eaten on Friday (2). The fruit eaten on Friday wasn't the banana (2), so the pear. Thus the banana was eaten on Thursday (2) and the peach on Wednesday (with almonds, above). The pecans weren't eaten on Thursday (4), so Friday. The walnuts were eaten on Thursday.

Thus:

Monday - pineapple - brazils;
Tuesday - apple - cashews;
Wednesday - peach - almonds;
Thursday - banana - walnuts;
Friday - pear - pecans.

No 92

Mitch has either the 4 or 6 of spades (clue 2) and a man who isn't Keith has either the 6 or 8 of spades. In other words, the 6 of spades is held by either Mitch or a man who isn't Keith. Thus Keith has the 4 of spades (clue 3) and Mitch has the 8 of hearts. Mitch has the 6 of spades (2). Keith has the 7 of diamonds (4), so the man with the 8 of spades has the 5 of diamonds (2). Keith has the king of hearts (4) and Neil has the jack of hearts, so Frank has the 10 of hearts. Frank has the 3 of diamonds (1), so Neil has the 8 of spades and 5 of diamonds (above). Mitch has the ace of diamonds and Frank has the queen of spades.

Thus (heart - diamond - spade):

Frank - 10 - 3 - queen;
Keith - king - 7 - 4;
Mitch - 8 - ace - 6;
Neil - jack - 5 - 8.

Solutions

No 93

The drawer with 18 screws in the bottom level isn't A (clue 4), so A in the bottom level has 30 screws (clue 1), A in the middle has 26, and D in the top has 28. The letter identifying the drawer with 16 in the top level and 22 in the middle (2) thus isn't A or D. D hasn't 32 in the middle (3), so 14. The drawer with 24 in the bottom level isn't B or C (3), so D. Drawer B has 18 in the bottom level (4), so C has 34. The letter identifying the drawers with 16 in the top and 22 in the middle thus isn't C (2), so B. C has 32 in the middle. C has 36 in the top (5) and A has 20 in the top level.

Thus (top - middle - bottom):
Drawer A - 20 - 26 - 30;
Drawer B - 16 - 22 - 18;
Drawer C - 36 - 32 - 34;
Drawer D - 28 - 14 - 24.

No 94

No clock stopped on either Tuesday or Saturday (grid). Thus either the carriage clock stopped on Wednesday and the grandfather clock stopped on Friday (clue 1) or the carriage clock stopped on Friday and the grandfather clock stopped on Sunday. In other words, the clock which stopped on Friday is either the carriage clock or the grandfather clock. So the wall clock stopped on Thursday (clue 3) and the clock which stopped at 6.30am did so on Wednesday. The carriage clock stopped at either 3.15am or 5.15pm (1), thus it stopped on Friday and the grandfather clock stopped on Sunday. So the grandfather clock stopped at

8.30pm (1) and the carriage clock stopped at 5.15pm. The alarm clock didn't stop at 6.30am (2), so the alarm clock stopped on Monday. The cuckoo clock stopped on Wednesday. The alarm clock didn't stop 7 hours earlier than the clock which stopped on Thursday (2), so the alarm clock didn't stop at 3.15am and the wall clock didn't stop at 10.15am. Thus the alarm clock stopped at 10.15am and the wall clock stopped at 3.15am.

Thus:
Alarm clock - 10.15am - Monday;
Carriage clock - 5.15pm - Friday;
Cuckoo clock - 6.30am - Wednesday;
Grandfather clock - 8.30pm - Sunday;
Wall clock - 3.15am - Thursday.

No 95

The Christmas pictures were taken in December (clue 2). From the listed years either the Christmas pictures were taken in 1989 and the birthday pictures in 1991 (clue 2) or the Christmas pictures were taken in 1994 and the birthday pictures in 1996. If the latter is true, then the pictures taken in March weren't of the concert (1), birthday party (3) or holiday (4), so the wedding. Then the 1986 event wasn't the concert (1) or the wedding (3), so the holiday, which (4) was in May: thus the wedding was in 1991 (3), so the concert was in 1989, which (1) isn't possible. So the Christmas pictures were taken in 1989 (2) and the birthday pictures in 1991. The September event wasn't the wedding (1) or birthday (3), so the

Solutions

concert. The concert wasn't in 1986 (1), so the 1991 pictures (birthday, above) weren't taken in July (3), so March. The wedding was in July. The holiday was in 1986 (3), so the wedding was in 1994 (1) and the concert was in 1996.

Thus:
Birthday - March - 1991;
Christmas - December - 1989;
Concert - September - 1996;
Holiday - May - 1986;
Wedding - July - 1994.